PART-TIME CURRENCY TRADER:

Trading Guide
For Working
Men & Women

By
Marquez Comelab

OrangesAndLime
Publishing

MELBOURNE

Copyright © 2005 by Marquez W. Comelab. All Rights Reserved.
Published by Oranges And Lime.

ISBN-13: 978-1-4116-8719-6
ISBN-10: 1-4116-8719-1

YOURS TO HAVE AND TO HOLD, BUT NOT TO COPY

No part of this publication may be reproduced, stored in a retrieval system or transmitted in any form or by any means: electronic, mechanical, photocopying, recording, scanning or otherwise, except as permitted under copyright laws in Australia, without the prior written permission of the author.

This publication is designed to provide accurate and authoritative information regarding the subject matter covered. It is sold with the understanding that the author is not engaged in rendering professional services. If professional advice or other expert assistance is required, the services of a competent professional person should be sought.

The material in this book is for educational purposes only. It should not be assumed that the methods, techniques, indicators, systems and strategies presented in this book will always be profitable or that they will not result in losses. Past results are not necessarily indicative of future results. Trading and investing are speculative and include risk of loss.

Hypothetical or simulated performance results have certain inherent limitations. Unlike an actual performance record, simulated results do not represent actual trading. Also, since the trades may not have been executed, the results may have under- or overcompensated for the impact, if any, of certain market factors, such as lack of liquidity. No representation is being made that any account will or is likely to achieve profits or losses similar to those shown.

EdNo. 220406

ACKNOWLEDGEMENTS

Thank you Nancy for being a loving wife who supports, helps, guides and encourages me in everything I do. You inspire me.

Thank you to my parents: Braulio and Mila Comelab; my parents-in-law: Ernest and Moysette Cauwels; and my brothers and sisters: Annaliese, Edward, Ellen and Vince – for their assistance, patience and understanding.

Finally, thank you to my friends who gave me the small pushes I needed to write a book for people like them who want to know more about trading. They are: James Ghidinelli, Sam Zarif, Ashwyn Gopalan, Lawrence Hammond, Mario Astorga, Kheen Gamboa, David Yip and Johan Alexander.

CONTENTS

CHAPTER 1: INTRODUCTION 1
    THE LANGUAGE 3
    HOW THIS BOOK IS ORGANISED 6

CHAPTER 2: FOREX TRADING 13
    THE FOREX (FX) MARKET: AN OVERVIEW 14
    WHO ARE THE MAIN 'PLAYERS' IN THIS 'PLAYGROUND'? 15
    WHAT CURRENCIES CAN YOU TRADE? 16
    WHY TRADE THE FOREX MARKET? 17

CHAPTER 3: THE BASIC CONCEPTS IN CURRENCY TRADING 23
    Price 23
    Spot Market 24
    Spot-Rate Quotation 24
    Margin Account / Trading Account / Equity Account 26
    Pips 26
    The Bid, The Offer/Ask, The Spread 27
    "Long" Vs "Short"; Trades Vs Positions 27
    Upward And Downward Trades 27
    How A Trade Works 28
    Calculating Profits or Losses In Terms Of The Quote Currency 29
    Round Trip Transactions 30
    Margin Ratio 30
    Margin Lending and Trading With Leverage 30
    Managing Risk By Using Stop-Loss Orders 32

CHAPTER 4: FINDING YOUR FOREX BROKER 35
    Avoiding Frauds And Scams 36
    Customer Service 39
    Software 39
    Data 40

Hours Of Operation *40*
Home Currency Feature *40*
Execution Speed Of Transactions *41*
Spread *41*
Timeframe *41*
Transaction Costs *42*
Minimum Opening Account Balance And Minimum Contract Sizes *42*
Margin Ratio *42*
Forums *43*
Interest *43*
Other Extras *43*
'Paper' Trading: Game Or Practice Accounts *44*

CHAPTER 5: WHY TRADERS FAIL AND HOW THIS BOOK MAY HELP 45

CHAPTER 6: PREPARATION 49
HOW CAN A TRADER PREPARE? 50
GETTING EDUCATED 50
PREPARING THE MIND 50
PREPARING YOUR FINANCES 58

CHAPTER 7: THE TRADING METHODOLOGY DEVELOPMENT PROCESS 63
THE TRADING METHODOLOGY DEVELOPMENT PROCESS 64

CHAPTER 8: ANALYSING THE MARKET: FUNDAMENTAL VS TECHNICAL ANALYSIS 71
FUNDAMENTAL ANALYSIS 72
TECHNICAL ANALYSIS 74
WHY I USE TECHNICAL ANALYSIS 76

CHAPTER 9: HOW TO 'READ' CHARTS 83
TIMEFRAME 83
VIEWING PRICE DATA: LINES, BARS AND CANDLES 84

HOW TO BUY AND SELL CURRENCIES: 'LONG' OR 'SHORT' POSITIONS 88

HOW TO IDENTIFY TRENDS 91

CHAPTER 10: HOW TO ANALYSE CHARTS USING 'CLASSICAL CHARTING' TECHNIQUES 97

THE FLEXIBILITY OF CLASSICAL CHARTING LINE TECHNIQUES 107

ENTERING TRADES USING CLASSICAL CHARTING 107

EXITING TRADES USING CLASSICAL CHARTING 109

CHAPTER 11: YOUR TOOLS, TECHNICAL INDICATORS 111

The Objectivity Of Indicators 111

Indicators Do Not Predict, They Measure 112

Simplicity Of Indicators 112

THE INDICATOR FAMILIES 112

Strengths & Weaknesses Of Indicators 137

Trading With Indicators 138

Fibonacci Numbers 139

Last Note About Indicators 140

CHAPTER 12: TRADING SYSTEMS 141

THE PSYCHOLOGICAL NEED FOR A TRADING SYSTEM 141

WHAT IS A TRADING SYSTEM? 144

THE REQUIREMENTS OF A TRADING SYSTEM 145

'Discretionary' Vs 'Mechanical' Rules 145

Counter-Trend And Trend-Following Systems 146

WHEN AND HOW TO ENTER THE MARKET 147

HOW TO EXIT A TRADE 149

ASSEMBLING YOUR TRADING SYSTEM 155

EXAMPLES OF TRADING SYSTEMS 158

SIMPLIFY YOUR SYSTEMS 167

OPTIMISATION AND CURVE FITTING 168

WHAT IS NEXT? 168

CHAPTER 13: TESTING TRADING SYSTEMS 169
- USING PAST DATA 169
- THE MEANS OF TESTING YOUR SYSTEM 171
- HOW TO CONDUCT YOUR EXPERIMENTS............................. 174

CHAPTER 14: POSITION-SIZING 185
- DISTINGUISHING BETWEEN POSITION-SIZING, RISK-MANAGEMENT & MONEY MANAGEMENT 185
- POSITION SIZING IS YOUR ARMOUR 186
- THE IMPORTANCE OF TRADING SMALL POSITIONS 186
- WHAT 'THE 1% RULE', MEANS 188
- HOW TO CALCULATE YOUR POSITION SIZE 190
- CALCULATING POSITION SIZE IF YOU DO NOT USE STOP LOSSES . 195
- RISK-MANAGEMENT STRATEGIES 195
- EXPLORING THE VARIABLES OF POSITION-SIZING 200

CHAPTER 15: DISCIPLINE & PSYCHOLOGY 207
- HOW AND WHY DO TRADERS DISOBEY THEIR SYSTEM?..... 208
- THE MINDSET OF A TRADER 212

CHAPTER 16: CLOSING REMARKS 223

APPENDICES 227
- APPENDIX A: IMAGES USED IN THIS BOOK.......................... 227

BIBLIOGRAPHY 229

INDEX 231

"Wealth is not measured by how much money we earn, or how much assets we have. It is measured by how much freedom we have to make the choices that are important to us: the freedom to choose where, how and why we live our lives."

– Marquez Comelab

CHAPTER 1: INTRODUCTION

We all have dreams. We all have a life we aspire to: a life that we may not be currently living. It may not necessarily be that the life we have is dreadful, but it is in our nature to look for ways to improve. We have commendable ideas and goals that we would like to achieve while we are still alive. For many, it is the lack of money that impedes our progress. We have commitments and there is a lot we have to do to survive. We go to work everyday. It is something we need to do so we might as well do it with happy spirits. But in our spare time, nothing stops us from exploring the possibilities of all that we can achieve and all that we can give to ourselves, to the people we love and to the world around us.

Right now, thousands of people are jotting down ideas, writing up plans, registering business names, creating web sites, writing, negotiating, selling, advertising and everything else that they need to do to realise their full potential as individual human beings. Many are drawn to various disciplines including the arts, business, politics, music, economics, science, mathematics, finance and many more. Personally, I am drawn towards trading the financial markets.

You can trade from anywhere in the world and you do not have to answer to anybody. The market provides a never-ending stream of opportunities for anyone to make money. It rewards individuals for their willingness to improve themselves, their ability to learn, think and exercise emotional control. It does not discriminate people because of their sex, the colour of their skin, the family they are born into or the religious beliefs they may hold.

The market provides a suitable environment where the attained level of success or failure is entirely attributed to the individual's character.

Money does not buy everything, but it buys what you need to live fully and enjoy your life. It gives you the power to be in places you would rather be and be with the people you care about most.

Trading is a craft and therefore, a trader needs a high level of success in order to be rewarded. Success in trading is not easy to come by. Studies have been conducted in the past to find out the success rates of traders. They all indicate that a great majority of traders have a high risk of ruin and only a relative few are able to make money from trading. Trading makes bankruptcy inevitable[1] and it is hazardous to your wealth[2].

A study of mutual fund investors made by Dalbar, Inc. from the USA, has pointed out that index funds and professional advisers beat amateur investors. The message is clear: the average investor is better off leaving his money with fund managers or with professionals. To some people who want to manage their own financial affairs, this may come as a disappointment. Metaphorically, I cannot apply a 'coat of sugar' to make this 'tablet of fact' any easier to 'swallow'. Therefore, any notion that trading is going to be an easy way to the 'good life' must be disturbed.

Trading is one of the hardest skills to master and it is not for those who do not have true passion for all that it entails. At the same time, however, I would not want you to dismiss the idea that trading is for you, without properly giving it some thought. If you are going to quit trading, then at least quit it for the right reasons.

Every endeavour has its own set of difficulties. Every journey has its own obstacles. Regardless of what it is that you want to do – be it starting a business or becoming a highly paid

---

[1] This comes from a report by Ronald L. Johnson prepared for the North American Securities Administrators Association (NASAA, a consumer protection group) on the success of retail traders.
[2] This is the conclusion made by Terry Odean, then a grad student at the University of California at Berkeley, and his Professor Brad Barber who researched a total of 76,465 discount-brokerage trading accounts between 1987 and 1996. Later, Odean repeated this study on a much larger scale, in the repeat he examined the accounts of 66,465 households from 1991 to 1996.

actor, doctor, or lawyer – there is always going to be competition. There is always going to be someone doing it better, faster and more efficiently than you.

Apart from providing the opportunity to establish a secure future and a life of abundance for you and your family, the market has a lot to offer in terms of what you can learn about yourself and how you experience the world. Unfortunately, research shows that most people enter the markets unprepared. They rush to the markets eagerly, without properly educating themselves. As a result, they take a quick series of losses and then leave with 'burnt fingers'. Despite this, these same researches also found that individuals who stick around to play the game longer can eventually become winners.

If you are reading this book secretly wishing that I have a magic secret or an astonishing get-rich-quick formula, I am sorry to tell you that I am but a poor and humble man. I have merely been fortunate to survive the on-going onslaught of the market long enough to have learnt the little that I understand now. I do know however, that had I known and understood many of these concepts when I began trading, my journey would have probably been a lot easier and a lot less frustrating. I have managed to trade this long without having experienced a series of catastrophic losses that would have wiped out any of my trading accounts. Therefore, I do believe the concepts I have written about in this book, are relevant and useful to anybody who has decided to take on whatever challenges trading the financial markets may bring.

THE LANGUAGE

GENDER

The English language is gender-specific. This brings forth a problem when a writer uses words like 'he', 'she', 'his', 'hers', 'him' and 'her'. Just for the sake of brevity, I sometimes automatically resort to using the male pronouns. No negative inference is made about the ability of women to trade. In fact, based on a study made on trading accounts[3], women are more successful in trading than men.

SPELLING

There are many types of English used all over the world. This book uses the Australian English, which has British, American and New Zealand influences. There are subtle differences between the way Australians spell to what you may normally be used to.

Australians use the letter '*u*'s in certain words. They use suffixes as *–ise* instead of *–ize* as well as *–t* instead of *–ed*. Here are examples of the common differences between how they spell words and how these words are *spelt* elsewhere.

	Australian Spelling	Other Known Spelling
1.	Centre	Center
2.	Endeavour	Endeavor
3.	Colour	Color
4.	Armour	Armor
5.	Dreamt	Dreamed
6.	Spelt	Spelled
7.	Learnt	Learned
8.	Jeopardise	Jeopardize
9.	Organise	Organize
10.	Organisation	Organization

TERMINOLOGY

When someone studies something for so long, they absorb many ideas and terminologies that permeate in the way that person uses language. Doctors, lawyers, mechanics, engineers and so on, often talk to people using phrases and words the average person does not use everyday. I will clarify some of the terminologies commonly used in this book to make it easier for all readers.

---

[3] A study made by Brad Barber and Terrance Odean.

Price

Price indicates the value of whatever it is that you are trading. If you are a share trader, the word price usually refers to the share price. In the foreign exchange market, the value of currencies is expressed in exchange rates. Therefore the words: price, value and exchange rates are used interchangeably depending on the context of their use.

Market: A Place

A market is where people go to buy and sell. In the physical world a market is a place. In trading, the market usually means the share market, the futures market, the options market or the currency market where you trade shares, futures, options and currencies respectively. These markets are not necessarily physical places. They may have exchanges but some, like the currency market, are simply a network of people from all over the world transacting from their offices, living rooms, airports and the like, using emails, telephones and websites to conduct transactions.

Market: A Herd Of People

As a trader, I may also write about 'the market' as an entity: as if it is alive. This is because many traders think of the market as a herd of people. It is the collective behaviour of this herd that makes up the behaviour of the market.

Bulls And Bears

Bulls are people who act on the belief that price will make an upward movement. They are the buyers in a market. Bears are people who act on the belief that price will make a downward movement. They are the sellers in a market.

Bullish And Bearish

Bullish may mean a few things:
- Something slanting upwards. For example: a bullish trend;
- Optimism;
- The value of a commodity is going to go up;

Bearish may mean a few things:
- Something slanting downwards. For example: a bearish trend;
- Pessimism;
- The value of a commodity is going to go down;

HOW THIS BOOK IS ORGANISED

I will now give you a run-down on how this book is organised. If you are already familiar with trading, then I leave it to you to skip the chapters you believe you will not need. However, when you do have the time, I recommend for you to go back to those parts and scan through them, just in case there are lessons you are yet to learn. To get the most of the information provided in this book, I would recommend you to read it in chronological order.

Chapter 2 – Forex Trading

Before we go through trading concepts, we need to discuss them in some form of context. I could have chosen to write this book as a general trading book; however, I decided to focus on providing examples of actual currency trading scenarios. The reason I choose to focus on the currency market is because it is the biggest market in the world and is fast becoming the trading vehicle for most private investors and traders alike. If you are happy trading shares, futures or options, the concepts in this book still apply. In this chapter, I will introduce the foreign exchange market to those of you who are not familiar with it.

Chapter 3 – The Basic Concepts Of Currency Trading

In this chapter, I outline the elementary ideas of currency trading so you know how a trade works and how you can make a profit or a loss from it. I will explain margin lending. If you are not familiar with the term, margin lending allows you to trade 50 to 400 times the size of your account. You will come to realise how you can effectively buy or sell 100,000 US Dollars by having only 500 US Dollars in your account.

Chapter 4 – Finding Your Forex Broker

You learn to do something by doing it so I need you to start trading, if you are not already doing so. I will help you find a broker that will suit your needs. I will run you through certain precautions to avoid fraud and scams and to help you set minimum expectations about costs, fees, software, data, transaction speed and other extra features and benefits that brokers are offering nowadays.

Chapter 5 – Why Traders Fail And How This Book May Help

Before you start trading, I will 'talk' about the four major reasons why most traders fail. Based from these, I will explain how this book may help overcome the problems and difficulties that people encounter while they are trading.

Chapter 6 – Preparation

We will discuss how to educate yourself and how to divide your financial resources before you start trading. Most importantly, I will touch on the consequences of the beliefs that some people may have about trading, about the market and about themselves; as well as their psychological qualities. We will consider how this may impact on your trading.

Chapter 7 – The Trading Methodology Development Process

When I began trading, I looked for a map that would give me a structure of how to organise all the information I had about trading. It took a long time for the lessons to sink in. In this chapter, I will demonstrate how to develop your own trading methodology based on how I develop mine. A trading methodology is not just about indicators, trading systems and position-sizing. It is a guideline of how a beginner may go about starting his or her own trading business. Equipped with this formula, novice traders would be able to speed up their learning a lot faster than I did.

Chapter 8 – Analysing The Market: Fundamental Vs Technical

In this chapter, I will discuss the two major means of analysing the market: fundamental and technical analysis. Fundamental analysis uses economic indicators to try to estimate the 'intrinsic' value of a currency and technical analysis uses charts, mathematics and statistics to trade the market. I will outline why I prefer technical analysis to help you decide which method would be right for you.

Chapter 9 – How To 'Read' Charts

The most essential skill in trading is the ability to read charts. Otherwise a trader would essentially be trading blind. In this chapter, I illustrate how to read charts and introduce close lines, bar charts and candlesticks. I will also show how to identify short-term trends and long-term trends using the Dow Theory: one of the most central doctrines in technical analysis.

Chapter 10 – How To Analyse Charts Using 'Classical Charting' Techniques

I will also demonstrate how you can analyse charts using the classical charting method – a method that does not need computers. All you need is a print-out of the chart, a ruler and a pencil. I will take you through how you may enter and exit trades using trend lines, trend channels as well as support and resistance levels.

Chapter 11 – Your Tools: Indicators

Instead of giving you a full index of all indicators, I will just give you a run-down of the most popular indicators that I use. I will outline trend-following indicators (moving average, dual moving average and the MACD) and sentiment-based oscillators (Stochastic, Williams%R and Commodities Channel Index). I will discuss their weaknesses, their strengths and how you can enter and exit a trade using their signals.

Chapter 12 – Trading Systems

After giving you an outline of indicators, I will explain how you can put them together to build your own trading system. I will discuss the psychological effects of trading without a system before I will make a distinction between discretionary systems from mechanical ones. We will touch on trend and counter-trend systems and how you can enter a trade using market orders, stop orders and limit orders. Apart from exiting using classical charting and indicators, I will also go through different ways in which you can exit trades when they go against you using various stop-loss mechanisms. After that, I will show you a few take-profit mechanisms which you can use to exit trades that turn out to be profitable. You will see how you can assemble a trading system from many various components. There are three trading systems given in this book. You may use or tweak them to make them your own.

Chapter 13 – Testing Trading Systems

After creating a trading system, you need to test it to assess whether it is likely to survive real-life market conditions. I am going to list the means with which you can test your system and show how you can get important statistical data about it. After you get your data, I will show you how you can calculate values, including your expected reward and your mathematical expectation of success. These numbers will help you assess the strength of your system if you keep trading it in the long run.

Chapter 14 – Position-Sizing

One of the biggest reasons traders lose a lot of money is because they do not know how to size their positions to minimise their risk and maximise the growth of their account. I will reveal to you something that is always so obvious that almost all novice traders miss it when they begin trading. Yet, it could be the key to their long-term survival. I will offer you a position-sizing formula which you can use to ensure that when you lose, you do not lose more than a particular percentage of your account. I will show you three different risk-management strategies and once you understand these, you can use their logic to create more complex ones in the future when you begin having more investors and more funds to trade with. We will also explore the different variables of position-sizing strategies by following a series of examples. You may come to realise certain relationships you did not know existed between risk, the growth of your trading money and your expectations.

Chapter 15 – Discipline & Psychology

As soon as traders start trading their systems, they will come to realise the hard-work is still not over. Most traders have problems following their own rules. In this chapter, we will examine how and why traders disobey their systems. I will take you through the operational, financial, psychological, health and life-related problems that traders face. After that, I will share with you the lessons I have learnt along the way and hopefully, they will help alleviate most of the psychological difficulties experienced by some traders.

Chapter 16 – Closing Remarks

CHAPTER 2: FOREX TRADING

You can know the rules of a game but before you can apply those rules you need to know what sport you will be playing. Therefore, before anything else, we need to choose what market we are going to trade. This way, I can explain the ideas we are covering in this book with actual trading scenarios.

There are many markets: markets to trade stocks, futures, options and currencies. These are the most accessible markets for everyday traders like you and I. People easily understand the basics of trading shares, so I will occasionally use examples from that market.

I began trading shares first and then I moved on to trading currencies. Therefore, most of the examples I will be using in this book are for trading currencies. Regardless of which market you want to trade and have access to, the concepts I outline in this book will still apply.

If you do not know a lot about currency trading, allow me to introduce it to you. It is what I trade and I believe that it is the best market to trade because of its efficiency. The transaction costs to carry out a trade are small and most brokers provide you with the tools and data you need to make your trading decisions. The market is open 24 hours a day which allows you to set your trading hours around your daily commitments. It is volatile, which is great for people who are looking for day-trading opportunities.

I will tell you what you need to know when you begin shopping around for a broker. I will guide you through how to avoid scams, and how you can assess the suitability of a particular broker.

IMPORTANT: If you are new to trading, I strongly recommend that you do not start trading with real money until you are familiar with why traders fail and how you can adequately prepare yourself. I will discuss this in Chapter 5.

THE FOREX (FX) MARKET: AN OVERVIEW

The foreign exchange market is the market in which you buy and sell currencies against one another. People may loosely refer to this market under different labels, including foreign exchange market, forex market, fx market or the currency market.

The foreign exchange market is the largest market in the world, with daily trading volumes over $1.5 trillion US dollars[4]. All transactions involving international trade and investment must go through this market because these transactions involve the exchange of currencies.

I consider it to be the most perfect market to trade because it has many buyers and sellers all trading the same products. There is a free flow of information and there are little barriers to participate.

The currency exchange market is an over-the-counter (OTC) market which means there is not one specific location where buyers and sellers can meet to exchange currencies. Instead, transactions are conducted by phone, fax, e-mail or through the websites of brokers who specialise in currency trading.

The major dealing centres at the time of writing are: London, with about 30% of the market; New York, with 20%; Tokyo, with 12%; Zurich, Frankfurt, Hong Kong and Singapore, with about 7% each, followed by Paris and Sydney with 3% each[5]. Since these centres are all over the world, foreign exchange traders can execute transactions 24 hours a day. The market only closes on the weekends.

---

[4] " Currency Market Overview."
Http://fxtrade.oanda.com/currency_trading/fxmarket.shtml (17th Dec. 2005).
[5] "Introduction to Currency Exchange and the FX Market."
http://fxtrade.oanda.com/currency_trading/intro_currency_exchange.shtml (17th Dec. 2005).

WHO ARE THE MAIN 'PLAYERS' IN THIS 'PLAYGROUND'?

The five broad categories of participants are: consumers, businesses, investors, speculators, commercial banks, investment banks and central banks.

Consumers, including visitors of countries, tourists and migrants, need to exchange currencies when they travel so they can buy local goods and services. These participants do not have the power to set prices. They just buy and sell according to the prevailing exchange rate. They make up a significant part of the volume traded in the market.

Businesses that import and export goods and services need to exchange currencies to receive or pay for goods bought or services rendered.

Investors and speculators need currencies to buy and sell investment instruments such as shares, bonds, bank deposits or real estate.

Large commercial and investment banks are the 'price makers'. They are the ones who buy and sell currencies at the bid-and-offer exchange rates that they declare through their foreign exchange dealers.

Commercial banks deal with customers on one hand, and with the Interbank or other banks, on the other hand. They profit by using the bid-and-offer spread[6]. They also make profits from speculating about whether the exchange rate will rise or fall.

Central banks engage in the foreign exchange market in their effective duty as banks for their particular government. They trade currencies not with the intention of making profits, but rather to facilitate government monetary policies and to help smoothen out the fluctuation of the value of their economy's currency.

---

[6] The bid price is the exchange rate at which the buyer is willing to buy and the offer price is the exchange rate at which the seller is willing to sell. The difference is called the bid-offer spread.

WHAT CURRENCIES CAN YOU TRADE?

You can trade any country's currency by exchanging it to another country's currency; however, the list below shows the ones that are most popular and that are made available by most online brokers for you to trade.

ISO[7]CODE	Currency	Symbol
AUD	Australian Dollar a.k.a. 'Aussie' or 'Oz'	A$
CAD	Canadian Dollar	Can$
CHF	Switzerland Franc a.k.a 'Swissi'	SwF
DKK	Denmark Krone	Dkr
EUR	European Dollar a.k.a 'Euro'	€
GBP	Great Britain Pound a.k.a 'Sterling' or 'Cable'	£
HKD	Hong Kong Dollar	HK$
JPY	Japanese Yen	¥
MXN	Mexican Peso	Mex$
NOK	Norway Krone	NKr
NZD	New Zealand Dollar a.k.a 'Kiwi'	NZ$
PLN	Poland Zloty	z dashed l
SAR	Saudi Arabia Riyal	SRls
SEK	Sweden Krona	kr or Sk
SGD	Singapore Dollar	S$
THB	Thailand Bhat	Bht or Bt
USD	United States Dollar	$
ZAR	South Africa Rand	R

NOTE:
Please note that from this point onwards, I refer to the names of these currencies using their ISO codes.

To trade the currencies above, you need to trade currency pairs. Think of these currency pairs as your trading instruments – instruments that you can buy or sell.

---

[7] ISO-International Organization for Standardization

Listed below are the most popular currency pairs that people trade:

1	AUD/JPY	Australian Dollar – Japanese Yen
2	AUD/USD	Australian Dollar – US Dollar
3	EUR/CHF	European Dollar – Switzerland Frank
4	EUR/GBP	European Dollar – Great Britain Pound
5	EUR/USD	European Dollar – US Dollar
6	EUR/JPY	European Dollar – Japanese Yen
7	GBP/CHF	Great Britain Pound – Switzerland Frank
8	GBP/USD	Great Britain Pound – US Dollar
9	USD/CAD	US Dollar – Canadian Dollar
10	USD/CHF	US Dollar – Switzerland Frank

You can exchange the currencies on the left for the currencies on the right.

WHY TRADE THE FOREX MARKET?

Historically, the FX market was available mostly to major banks, multinational corporations and other participants who traded in large transaction sizes and volumes. Small-scale traders – including individuals like you and I – had little access to this market for a very long time. Now with the advent of the Internet and technology, FX trading is becoming an increasingly popular investment alternative for the public.

The benefits of trading the currency market are the following:
1. It is open 24-hours and it closes only on the weekends,
2. It is liquid and efficient,
3. It is volatile,
4. It has low transaction costs,
5. You can use a high level of leverage (borrowed money) with ease and
6. You can profit from a bull or a bear market.

Continuous, 24-Hour Trading

The currency exchange is a 24-hour market. You may decide to trade after you come home from work. Regardless of what time-frame you want to trade, there would be enough buyers and sellers to take the other side of your trade. This feature of the market gives you enough flexibility to manage your trading around your daily routine.

Liquidity And Efficiency

When there are many buyers and many sellers, you can expect to buy or sell at a price that is close to the last market price. Liquidity or market liquidity refers to the capacity to buy or sell a particular item or commodity without causing a significant movement in the price. The currency market is the most liquid[8] market in the world. Trading volume in the currency markets can be between 50 and 100 times larger than the New York Stock Exchange[9].

When you are trading stocks, you may experience events where one piece of news lifts or depresses the price of the underlying stock you may have bought into. Perhaps a director is kicked out by the shareholders of a company or the company has just released a new product and big investors are buying the shares of a particular company. The actions or inactions of one or more individuals can drastically affect the share prices. So if you are relying on television reports and newspapers to get your news, most of the opportunities or warnings will have come too late for you to take timely action.

The value of currencies on the other hand is affected by so many factors and so many participants that the likelihood of any one individual or group of individuals drastically affecting the

---

[8] Liquidity or Market Liquidity – Market liquidity refers to the ability to quickly buy or sell a particular item or commodity without causing a significant movement in the price.

[9] "Benefits of Currency Trading vs. Equity Trading" Http://fxtrade.oanda.com/currency_trading/fx_vs_equity.shtml (17th Dec. 2005).

value of a currency is minute. The currency market is hard to manipulate because of its sheer size. The ability for people to engage in 'insider trading' is almost eliminated. As an average trader, you are less disadvantaged. You are likely to be playing on equal ground with all the other traders and investors whom you are competing against.

Note About Price Gaps:
For those people who have already traded other markets, you probably know about price 'gaps'. 'Gaps' occur when prices 'jump' from one price level to another without having taken any incremental steps to get there. For example, you may be trading a share that closes at $10 at the end of today and because of some event that happens overnight; it opens tomorrow at $5 and continues to go downwards for the rest of the day.

Gaps bring about another degree of uncertainty that may meddle with a trader's strategy. Probably one of the most worrying aspects of this is when a trader uses stop-losses. In this case, if a trader puts a stop-loss at $7, his trade will remain open overnight and the trader wakes up tomorrow with a loss bigger than he was prepared for.

After looking at a couple of forex charts, you will realise there are little price 'gaps' or none at all, especially on the longer-term charts like the 3-hour, 4-hour or the daily charts.

Volatility

Trading opportunities exist when prices fluctuate. If you buy a share for $2 and it stays there, there is no opportunity to make a profit. The magnitude of this fluctuation and its frequency is referred to as volatility. As a trader, it is volatility that you profit from. Large volume transactions and high liquidity combined with fewer trading instruments produce great intraday volatility in the currency market which day-traders can exploit. The high volatility of the currency market suggests that a trader can potentially earn more money from currency trading than trading the most liquid shares[10]. For this reason, currencies make a better trading vehicle for day-traders than the equity markets.

Low Transaction Costs

A currency transaction typically incurs no commission or transaction fees. For a forex trader, the spread is the only cost he or she needs to cover in taking on a position. In addition, because of the currency market's efficiency, there are little or no 'slippage' costs[11]. Individuals can trade more frequently at small costs because of lower transaction costs, minimum slippage and strong intraday volatility. As an estimate, you may only expect to have a spread of 0.03% of your position size. To give you an example, you can buy and sell 10,000 US Dollars and this will only incur a 3-point spread, equivalent to $3.

Leverage

When you are trading shares, there are not many banks or people who would lend you money to trade. Even if there are, it would be hard for you to convince them to invest in you and in your idea that a certain share is going to go up or down. Therefore, most of the time, if you have a $10,000 account, you can only afford to buy $10,000 worth of stocks.

---

[10] Ibid.

[11] Slippage is the cost involved when traders enter the market at a price worse than the level they wanted to get into. For example, a trader wants to buy a share at $2.00 but by the time the order gets executed, he gets to buy the shares at $2.50. That fifty cents difference is his slippage cost. Slippage cost affects large-volume traders a lot. When they buy large quantities of a commodity, it oversupplies the market with buy orders. This applies a pressure for the price to go up. By the time they finish buying all the quantities they wanted, the average price they get would be higher than the price they wanted. Conversely, when they sell large quantities of a commodity, they oversupply the market with sell orders. This applies a pressure for the price to go down. By the time they finish selling, their average selling price is less than what they initially intended to sell them for.

In currency trading however, because you use 'borrowed money', you can trade $10,000 of a currency and you only need anywhere between fifty[12] to two hundred dollars[13] in your trading account. This makes it possible for an average trader with a small trading account, under $10,000 to profit enough from the movements of the currency exchange rates. I will explain more of this concept in chapter 3.

Profit From A Bull And Bear Market

When you are trading shares, you can only profit when the price of a stock goes up. When you suspect that it is about to go down or that it is just going to move sideways, the only choice you have is to sell your shares and stand aside. One of the frustrations of trading shares is that an individual cannot profit when prices are going down. In the currency market, it is easy for you to trade a currency downward so you can profit when you think it is going to lose value. This is easy to do because currency trading simply involves buying one currency and selling another, there is no structural bias that makes it difficult to trade 'downwards'. This is why the currency market has been occasionally referred to as the eternal bull market.

---

[12] For a margin lending ratio of 200:1.
[13] For a margin lending ratio of 50:1.

CHAPTER 3: THE BASIC CONCEPTS IN CURRENCY TRADING

If you are new to currency trading, this chapter covers its most basic concepts. I will need you to scan this chapter so you can be conversant on the topic and to prepare yourself for the subsequent chapters.

Price

In the share market, the price of the instrument (that is the share) you are trading is plotted like this:

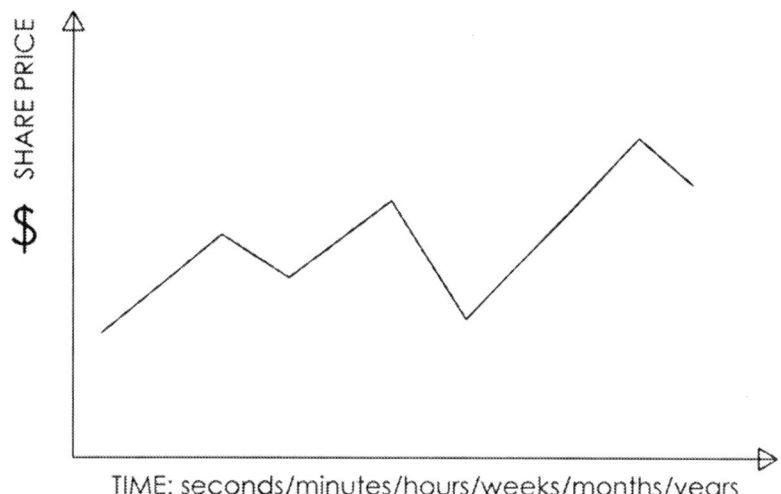

Image 1: Plotting Share Prices

When you are trading currencies, the price of a currency is expressed in terms of its value to another currency; therefore, you can draw its prices on a chart like this:

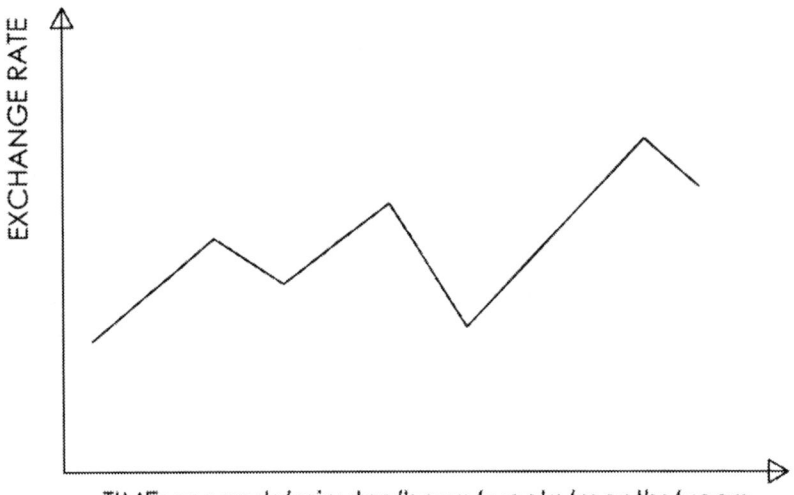

Image 2: Plotting Forex Prices

Spot Market

Please note that the examples in this book are based on spot market transactions. A spot market transaction occurs when two parties agree to exchange currencies within the settlement date (2 business days) at an exchange rate they agree on today. Traditional spot transactions required actual exchanges of currencies. Nowadays, speculators do not need to exchange currencies physically.

Spot-Rate Quotation

"The spot exchange rate is the price of one currency in terms of another for immediate delivery. The value of a commodity traded (*the base currency*) is a currency expressed in terms of another

currency (*the quote currency*)[14]." The exchange rate between two currencies *x* and *y* can be expressed in two ways:
   a) The direct method – also known as the 'price quotation', and
   b) The indirect method – also known as the 'quantity quotation'

The Direct Quotation – Price Quotation

Quotation format: *quote currency / base currency;*
The quote currency is what you get in exchange for one unit of the base currency.

For example:

USD/AUD = 0.77 is the same as AUD/USD = 1.30 if quoted using direct quotation. They both infer that 1 AUD buys 0.77 USD or that 1 USD sells for 1.30 AUDs.

The Indirect Quotation – Quantity Quotation

Quotation format: *base currency / quote currency;*
The quote currency is what you get in exchange for one unit of the base currency.

For example:

AUD/USD = 0.77 is the same as USD/AUD = 1.30 if quoted using the indirect quotation. They both infer that 1 AUD buys 0.77 USDs or that 1 USD sells for 1.30 AUDs.

PLEASE NOTE: I have given both formats to provide you with more flexibility when you are dealing with brokers from all over the world who may use one of the two formats. **I will be using the indirect or the quantity quotation from here onwards** because

---

[14] Moosa, Imad A. *International Finance* (1998), p7.

that is what my broker uses and it seems to be the more common format online. This is because at the time of writing, there are more online brokers based in the USA – where the indirect quotation is common-practice – than anywhere else in the world.

Margin Account / Trading Account / Equity Account

To begin your currency trading business, you need to open an account with a broker. In numerous books and computer programs, this will be referred to as your margin account as well as your trading account or your equity account. Money is deposited to your account when you close a profitable trade. Money is deducted from your account when you close a losing trade. The objective of the trading game is simply to close profitable trades because every time that happens, you get money in your account.

In the equities market when you buy 10,000 shares at $1.00 each, you need $10,000 in your account. When you trade currencies, you are trading a margin account. You are effectively buying and selling with borrowed money so every dollar in your margin account can control as much as 400[15] times its value.

Pips

A pip is the smallest movement available in any currency instrument. Most currency pairs are quoted using 5 basis points, with each basis point equal to 0.0001. A quotation that includes the Yen is quoted in 3 basis points, with each basis point being 0.01.

To illustrate this idea: the difference between AUD/USD = 0.7566 and AUD/USD = 0.7567 is 1 pip only. The difference between GBP/JPY = 199.62 and GBP/JPY = 199.64 is 2 pips.

---

[15] This depends on the margin ratio being offered by your broker. 400:1 margin ratio is the highest, the author have been made aware of.

The Bid, The Offer/Ask, The Spread

The Bid is the price at which buyers offer to buy currencies. The Offer, also known as the *Ask*, is the price at which sellers offer to sell their currencies. Think of it this way: Bid to buy, Offer to sell. The spread is the difference between the two.

For example: if your broker has a bid-ask quote on the AUD/USD as: 0.7560 / 70, this means that buyers can buy 1 AUD at 0.7570 USDs. Sellers can sell 1 AUD at 0.7560 USDs.

Therefore if you buy and sell 1 AUD simultaneously, you would have lost 10 pips. This 10 pip difference is referred to as the 'spread'. Who pockets this? Your broker does. This is how they make their living. The 'spread' is a cost that you incur as a trader for using the services of your broker.

"Long"Vs "Short"; Trades Vs Positions

Consider a trader who thinks the USD will appreciate over the JPY. Currently the USD/JPY is 112.45. What he would like to do is to buy US Dollars and sell the JPYs because he thinks the USD is going to get relatively stronger over the JPY. In other words, he is taking a 'long' position on the USD and a 'short' position on the JPY. The trader needs to open a 'long' trade on the USD/JPY to take action on this set of beliefs.

If however, the trader believes the USD will depreciate over the JPY, then he needs to sell USDs and buy JPYs. In other words, he is taking a 'short' position on the USD and a 'long' position on the JPY. The trader needs to open a 'short' trade on the USD/JPY.

Upward And Downward Trades

Buying, selling, going 'long' and going 'short' are industry terms. To make it easier, I may refer to 'long' trades as upward trades and 'short' trades as downward trades.

How A Trade Works

I will now take you through two simple trades so you can see how you can make or lose money in trading currencies WITHOUT using a broker.

Trade 1: When The Home Currency Is One Of The Currency Pairs Being Traded

Bob, an American trader (therefore USD is his home currency), thinks the Australian Dollar is going to appreciate relative to the US Dollar. Currently, the AUD/USD is quoted at a buying price of 0.7566. He buys 10,000 AUDs. This costs him $7566[16] USDs. After five minutes the AUD/USD is quoted at a selling rate of 0.7576[17]. He sells his $10,000 AUDs and he gets paid $7,576USDs. He gains $10[18] USDs in his bank account.

Trade 2: When The Home Currency Is Not One Of The Currency Pair Being Traded

The next trade Bob thinks the GBP will appreciate relative to the JPY. GBP/JPY is currently quoted at 199.62. He buys 10,000 GBPs in exchange for 1996200[19] JPYs. Five minutes later, the GBP/JPY rate increased to 199.82. He sells his GBPs in exchange for 1998200[20] JPYs. He just gained 2,000 JPYs. Since he lives in the US, his home currency is US Dollars. He needs to convert 2000 JPYs to USDs. Currently, the USD/JPY exchange rate is 112.45. So when he exchanges his 2000 JPYs, he gets 17.78[21] USDs in his account.

---

[16] 10,000 x 0.7566 = 7566
[17] 10,000 x 0.7576 = 7576
[18] 7576 − 7566 = 10
[19] 10,000 x 199.62 = 1,996,200
[20] 10,000 x 199.82 = 1,998,200
[21] 2,000 / 112.45 = 17.78

With technology and the Internet, these types of transactions are so simple to do. Nowadays, opening and closing a trade usually takes one click of your mouse. Your broker's online system will conduct the rest of the transaction for you. It is all instantaneous. Money transfers from one currency to another in small electronic pulses over the Internet.

Calculating Profits or Losses In Terms Of The Quote Currency

To summarise the mathematics above, this is how you calculate your profits or losses in terms of the quote currency:

$P = SU - BU$

Where:
      B = Buying Price,
      S = Selling Price,
      U = Units to Trade,
      P = Profits in terms of the quote currency.

Similarly, this transposes to…

$P = U(S-B)$

Using the second trade example above where we are trading the GBP/JPY, we know the following:
      $B = 199.62$
      $S = 199.82$
      $U = 10,000$

We use the formula: $P = U(S-B)$.

We substitute the values:
$P = 10000 * (199.82 - 199.62)$
$P = 10000 * (0.20)$
$P = 2000$ JPYs

Since the trader is an American, he needs to convert the 2000JPYs to his home currency. The USD/JPY exchange rate is currently 112.45; therefore, his gain is 17.79USDs. This is calculated as 2000JPYs / 112.45 = 17.79 USDs.

Round Trip Transactions

Unlike the traditional method of trading currencies, speculative trading is referred to as a 'round trip' transaction because the positions will be closed (settled) within the same account and in the same currency from which the trades originated. This makes it possible for speculative traders to make money from exchange rate movements without having to exchange currencies.

Margin Ratio

Margin ratio is the ratio between how much you can effectively borrow for every dollar you have in your margin account. You use this borrowed money to take on positions. A 200:1 margin ratio means that for every dollar you have in your margin account, you can buy or sell $200. Thus, if you have $100 USDs in your account, you can effectively control $20,000 USDs to exchange with another currency.

Margin Lending and Trading With Leverage

Online Internet Brokers now make margin lending easy. This means that they will effectively lend you money so you can play in the currency markets. A trader like Bob from the example above can benefit from this development. If you trade currencies the traditional way like Bob did, you would have needed at least $7,566 USDs in your bank account to buy $10,000 AUDs.
	Nowadays, if you sign up for an account with a forex broker, you do not need $7566 USDs to buy 10,000 AUDs. I will now explain to you how this works in a way that, hopefully, simplifies the idea.

What brokers do is this: if you want to buy 10,000AUDs the broker will 'effectively'[22] lend you the money needed to buy 10,000 AUDs. All they need you to do is to open a margin account with them.

Assume that you open a $10,000 margin account with a broker who offers you a 200:1 margin ratio[23]. You deposit this money to a separate bank account the broker has set aside for its clients. You open a 'long' trade on the AUD/USD to buy 10,000 AUDs. Your broker will then hold $50[24] from your margin account during the duration of that trade. Brokers normally refer to this $50 as your margin for that trade. You now have $9,950 available margin. You can buy another 10,000 AUDs if you want and they will just hold on to another $50 margin for that trade. If this is the case, then your broker would have set aside, $100[25] as your margin. You are controlling 20,000 USDs and you still have $9,900 available in your margin account.

You can think of this $100 margin the broker holds for you as your deposit. In a way, your broker needs this for security just in case you fail to close your trades when the market adversely goes against your trade.

Let's say the AUD/USD has gone up and the selling rate is now 10 pips away from the rate you bought it at. You close the trade. You make a 10 pip profit. A 10 pip profit in this $20,000 total position size would make you $20[26] USDs. As soon as you close the trade, your broker will release the $100 margin that he held for you and make it part of your available margin again. Therefore, after you have closed your two trades, you would have $10,020 in your margin account. Had you made a 10 pip loss on the trade, you would have $9,980 in your margin account. Further, had the AUD/USD gone down by 66 pips to 0.7500 from 0.7566, you would have made a loss of $132[27] in five minutes. Of course the reverse is true if you made 66 pips profit.

---

[22] I use the word 'effectively' because no money is transferred physically or electronically.
[23] A 200:1 margin ratio means that you can take a position that is 200 times greater than your margin availability.
[24] 10,000 / 200 = 50
[25] 50 x 2 = 100
[26] (20,000 x 0.7576) – (20,000 x 0.7566) = 20
[27] (20,000 x 0.7500) – (20,000 x 0.7566) = -$132

WARNING:

By having the ability to trade with 'borrowed' money, you are magnifying your potential gain from a trade if the trade is profitable. But what is important to know is that by doing this, you are also worsening your potential loss if the trade becomes a losing trade.

If you do not understand this already, please make sure that you do so you can trade responsibly. Many people who trade 'leveraged' markets end up risking too much, not because trading is dangerous, but because they do not understand this concept. I would not want you to lose all your money on only one, two or three trades. It is important for you to read the chapter on position-sizing and risk-management because I will delve into this danger a lot more.

Managing Risk By Using Stop-Loss Orders

The best way for you to protect yourself from potential mishaps is to set stop-losses as soon as you enter a trade. All brokers have a feature on their website that allows you to set your stop-loss. If yours does not, then you are not dealing with a responsible broker. A stop-loss is a rate that you set so once the exchange rate touches it; you are ordering your broker to close that particular trade. For example, you open a $20,000 'long' trade on the AUD/USD at a rate of 0.7566 and it goes down to 0.7000. You have a stop-loss set at 0.7500 which means you would have only lost 66 pips ($132) instead of 566 pips ($1,132[28])!

Most brokers manage risk by reducing their margin ratio so more of your money will be set aside for each trade that you open. They also manage risk by implementing rules for a margin call when your losses get too big. A margin call is a warning from your broker that you need to add more funds to your margin account or close some of your existing trades. If you do not, they will close all your trades. Low margin ratios and margin calls are there to protect them and to protect you from trading dangerously.

---

[28] (20,000 x 0.7000) – (20,000 x 0.7566) = -$1132

I believe the most effective way for most people to learn any skill is by doing it. One cannot learn how to drive simply by reading books about driving. Therefore, now that I have explained the basic concepts of trading currencies, you will need to start looking for a broker so you can start trading with 'fake' or real money.

> "For the things we have to learn before we can do them, we learn by doing them."
>
> — Aristotle (384 BC - 322 BC), *Nichomachean Ethics*

CHAPTER 4: FINDING YOUR FOREX BROKER

A broker is an individual or a firm that executes buy and sell orders submitted by an investor. Your broker is going to be your business partner. His strengths will be an advantage for you and his weaknesses will limit you. So choose your broker wisely before you start trading with real money.

The best and probably the only place you will ever need to look for a broker is on the Internet. Just go to your favourite search engine and search for the key words: forex, foreign exchange, trading currencies, fx trading and fx brokers. This should be enough to give you a long list of brokers. When you click around their websites, bear in mind a few things:

- Frauds and scams,
- Customer service,
- Software,
- Data,
- Hours of operation,
- Home currency feature,
- Execution speed of transactions,
- Spread,
- Chart time-frames,
- Transaction costs,
- Minimum opening account balance,
- Margin ratio,
- Forums,
- Interest,

- Other extras and
- Game or practice accounts.

Avoiding Frauds And Scams

Many people have been 'burnt' from scams on the Internet. Some brokerage sites may look so legitimate that you doubt whether they would have gone through all that trouble building a trading platform just to 'steal' your money. Beware.

Find out where the broker is based. If I find that they are based in a country where the financial industry is, in my opinion, rather unregulated and underdeveloped, I quickly forgo signing up. This is terrible news for honest brokers in those countries, but your job as a trader is to protect your capital. If you lose that, then you cannot trade. The onus is on them to convince you that they will do what is right for you as an investor.

I started out with an Australian broker. Currently I am using an American one. I have not tried UK-based brokers but the British financial industry is trustworthy. Companies in countries such as Japan, Germany and France are just as good if their website speaks your language.

Notice any licence numbers that they may have registered with regulatory bodies that act like government watchdogs who oversee the finance and investments industries. These are organisations that impose strict rules to safeguard your investments[29]. Take note there are some fake regulatory bodies mentioned in cyber-space as well[30]. Take a look at how long they have been operating. Try to search out any reviews or comments made about them. See if you can find forums where traders have discussions about their brokers.

---

[29] Some of these rules may include the requirement that brokers segregate all customer funds from the operational funds of the business. Your money is required to be put in highly-reputable banks and the funds are only withdrawn from these accounts upon specific withdrawal requests.

[30] Go to http://www.marquezcomelab.com/, where I will be posting some of the ones I have come across.

Below is a list of pointers to keep in mind to help you avoid being a victim of a scam:

1. **Stay Away From Opportunities That Sound Too Good To Be True**

There are people who may have acquired a large sum of money recently and who are shopping around for safe investment vehicles. These may include retirees who have access to their retirement funds. It is understandable why retirees would be drawn to 'high-return, low-risk investments'. This is also what makes them vulnerable. If you identify yourself to be one of these people, be careful. Many deceitful characters are after your money. Further, only allocate a tiny amount of your money to trading until you can start growing it. Not all people can trade successfully, so it is a venture you should take on haphazardly. It is your life savings at risk.

2. **Avoid Individuals Or Organisations Who Claim To Predict Or Guarantee Large Profits**

Any form of trading is hard. Trading currencies is no different. Be wary of statements that make it sound easy:
- "Whether the market moves up or down, in the currency market you will make a profit";
- "Make $1000 a week, every week";
- "We are outperforming 90% of domestic investments";
- "You'll make returns of 70% a year" or
- "Here is a no-risk strategy".

If they could make such returns, why would they even bother letting you know about it?

3. **Be Wary Of Companies Who Downplay Investment Risks**

Hold your wallet tight and zip up your purse when companies say that written risk disclosure agreements are routine formalities imposed by the government. Watch out for the following statements:

- "With a $10,000 deposit, the maximum you can lose is $200 to $250 a day";
- "We promise to recover any losses you have".

4. Be Wary Of Companies That Claim To Trade In The 'Interbank Market'

Do not believe it when some people say that they have access to the 'Interbank market' or that they can give you access to trade in that market because that's where you can get bargain prices. This is not true. The 'interbank market' is not a place: it is not a physical building. It is simply a loose network of currency transactions negotiated between big financial institutions and other large companies.

5. Ethnic Minorities Are Often Targeted

Ethnic newspapers and television 'infomercials' are sometimes used to attract Russian, Chinese and Indian minorities. These ads offer so-called 'job opportunities for account executives to trade foreign currencies', whereby the recruited 'account executive' is expected to use his own money to trade currencies. They are often encouraged to recruit members like their friends and family to do the same.

6. Seek Out The Company's Background

Check any information you receive to be sure the company is who they claim to be. If possible, try to get the background of the people running the company. Do not rely solely on verbal statements and promises made by the company's employees.

7. If You Are In Doubt, It Is Not Worth Risking Your Money

If after trying to request information and at the end of it all, you are still in doubt about the credentials of a particular company, my suggestion is to start looking elsewhere.
    You may find further information by contacting government 'watchdogs' because they keep up to date with trends

and reports about scams and other fraudulent activities. I know that in the US, they have The United States Commodity Futures Trading Commission (CFTC). Australians have the Australian Securities and Investments Commission (ASIC). I have posted the watchdogs of other countries on my website:
http://www.marquezcomelab.com.

I will also keep you up to date with information on the brokers that I think are worth your time researching. I will be posting information on the latest trends and scams I may become aware of, so make sure to check the website every now and then.

Customer Service

Browse their websites, find out as much as you can and if you have any questions that are not answered, do not be afraid to call them, or to contact them by e-mail. Notice how they respond to you. Assess their professionalism. Keep in mind how quickly they respond, how well they answer your query and how keen they are in helping you out. Many brokers have helpful staff. Most make the effort to call you even if you live abroad. If you do not feel that they are being helpful at all, forget about them. You are a potential client and if they do not attend to your needs now, what makes you think they will in the future? If they have not responded in a week, you should scratch them off your list.

Software

Some brokers require you to download their trading platform to your computer. The advantages of these systems are that they typically have lot of useful features. It may also be possible for you to store a large amount of historical data on your computer's hard disk, which would allow you to do your analysis when you are not connected to the Internet.

Other brokers do not need you to install anything on your computer. They have designed their platform so it can be loaded by any popular Internet browser. These are usually small applications that load quickly. You can go to any Internet café, anywhere in the world, and you can trade your account. The downfall of these types of platforms is that you cannot analyse your data while you are not connected to the Internet.

Data

Some brokers offer quotes that are delayed by 20 minutes. If you are planning to trade daily or weekly, this may not be a problem; however, intraday trading requires real-time data.

You also need to look at the quality and the quantity of any historical price data a broker provides for free. You need historical data to test your strategies later on. Since forex is not a centralised market, brokers and data providers do not have the same exact price data. It makes it even more important that the broker provides you with his own data. When you test your system with data acquired from one source and then actually trade a platform with different data, your profit projections might not be as accurate and your results may vary, drastically.

Hours Of Operation

You need to make sure the broker is able to take your trade when you want to trade.

Home Currency Feature

Choose a broker that can work with the same currency as your home currency. If you choose a broker from a country with a different currency to your home currency, then this is a big factor for you. It is not only because it is inconvenient and time-consuming, but because it impacts on your trading results.

Consider the following example: Emma is an Australian trader who has a trading system that can grow her money at an average rate of 20% a year. She deposits 10,000 AUDs to her broker's account in the USA. At the time, the AUD/USD exchange rate was 0.7700. So her money got converted to 7,700 USDs. She trades this account and manages to grow her money by 20% to 9,240 USDs. That's a profit of $1540 USDs for that year. Within that time, however, the AUD/USD had gone up to 0.9000. If she exchanges her money back to her Australian bank account, she will only receive 10,267 AUDs. That is a growth of only 2.67% instead of 20%.

Of course the exchange rate could have gone the other way which would have worked better for Emma; however, the point is that being in this position will affect your performance as a trader.

Execution Speed Of Transactions

You must be able to execute and complete orders immediately. Most, if not all, brokers can do this. Avoid brokers who cannot.

Spread

Like I wrote in the previous chapter, the spread is the difference between the buying rate and the selling rate. If the GBP/JPY has a bid-ask rate of 199.62/65 then the broker is making a three-pip spread on the transaction. A broker can sell Sterlings to you at an exchange rate of 199.65 and at the same time buy the same amount of Sterlings at an exchange rate of 199.62. It is the broker's job to make sure that his business survives by making sure he profits enough from spreads; however, it is your job to minimise the cost of the 'spread' for you. So shop around for brokers who can offer you the smallest spread you can find. Even after you have signed up with a broker, continue to shop around ever so often.

Timeframe

The forex market has enough liquidity and volatility for you to try and day-trade it. You can choose to trade 1-minute, 5-minute, 15-minute, 30-minute, 1-hour, 3-hour and 4-hour charts. You can also trade daily, weekly or monthly.

Transaction Costs

There are many good brokers out there now that do not charge any monthly fees, sign-up costs or subscription fees of any sort. They provide you with the historical data, news, tools and information, with free use of their platform. The industry is very competitive for brokers. Unless they provide any additional or unique features with their platform that distinguishes them from their competitors, the only operational cost you should expect to incur is the spread.

Minimum Opening Account Balance And Minimum Contract Sizes

Brokers used to allow only a minimum contract size of $100,000. This was the standard. That means that you have to buy or sell $100,000 worth of currencies to trade. Trading this big means that every pip a currency pair makes would have a $10 effect on a trader's account. A 300-pip movement against a trader's position within a day would mean a $3000 drop in the value of his margin accounts. It is not for the lightly-financed private trader.

Brokers have introduced mini-accounts where the minimum contract size is just $10,000. This made it easy for people to open a margin account for as little as $1,000. A 300-pip movement against a trader's position in one day would only mean a $300 loss. That is a lot more manageable than $3,000.

I know of a broker who offers a contract size of only one dollar! If you are comparing between two evenly-matched brokers you should go for the broker that offers you a smaller minimum contract size. In Chapter 14, I will explain how this helps in your position-sizing and how crucial it is for your trading survival.

Margin Ratio

You should be all right as long as your broker offers you a choice of margin ratio that lies within the 20:1 to 400:1 margin ratio. When you begin trading though, I would probably recommend that whenever possible, you start trading at a low setting of around 20:1 to 100:1. You can adjust this just as soon as you start finding out more about trading. For now, this will ensure that you do not risk too much and that you do not open too many positions. Trading a position size that is too big is dangerous, because any adverse movement in the market can put a large dent on your margin account; while taking too many positions at once, spreads out your focus. This reduces the quality of your planning and your analysis.

Forums

It is good if a broker provides his own forum where users can have discussions about trading in general and about trading with that particular broker. It is good to see if you can find people openly criticising or praising the broker. You can get a good gauge of the broker's strengths and weaknesses this way. It is also a sign the broker is not afraid to improve himself by being open to feedback.

Interest

Take a look if your broker pays you interest on your margin account. Find out how often the interest is calculated and how often it is paid. This is a good-to-have extra. Personally though, if you are opening a trading account simply to make interest revenue, you are better off putting your money into something as simple as a savings account. Do not choose a broker simply for this reason.

Other Extras

Take a look if your broker offers you free access to market news, research, commentaries and economic calendars. If your trading style requires these extras, then you need to ensure that you have access to these extras at a minimised cost.

'Paper' Trading: Game Or Practice Accounts

Once you find a broker who accommodates for your needs, you will have the opportunity to open a practice account: an account that trades with fake money. The purpose of this is for you to get used to the trading platform of that particular broker. Each trading platform may be different.

At the most basic level, you need to know how the broker wants you to put orders and how his system carries them out. Put in a few trades and watch them. As your trades make profits or losses, notice how all the other numbers on the trading platform change as well. Notice how much margin dollars they are holding from your account for every trade that you put in. You learn more than just about your broker's platform. You also learn about trading. You learn about currencies. Best of all, you can get all this knowledge free.

Apart from giving you the opportunity to learn how to carry out trades and how to read all the symbols, graphs and numbers on the platform, a practice account allows you to 'paper trade' the market.

Paper trading refers to the practice of trading the markets with pretend money. I encourage you to do this in your early stages while you are putting together ideas on how you can trade successfully.

I strongly recommend that you continue improving your method until it starts becoming profitable before you trade with real money. The idea of this is to allow you to develop your trading ideas first before you start dealing with the psychological elements of trading.

Your broker will provide you with the access and the facilities to trade currencies in the foreign exchange market. Once you have opened and deposited money into an account, you can start trading. Before you start trading however, I strongly recommend that you read through the next chapter.

CHAPTER 5: WHY TRADERS FAIL AND HOW THIS BOOK MAY HELP

From my research and personal experience, the most common reasons people lose money trying to trade the financial markets are as follows:

1. The lack of adequate financial and psychological preparation;
2. The failure to develop a methodical approach to trade the markets;
3. The failure to understand the concepts of position-sizing and how it impacts on managing money and managing risks;
4. The lack of discipline to follow through detailed plans and the failure to understand how their emotional and psychological needs interfere with their performance.

This is going to set out the structure of this book from here onwards. I will start off by tackling many of the preconceived notions, attitudes, beliefs and other psychological qualities that some novices may have about themselves and the market. All of these have the potential to lead them into some of the psychological pitfalls that are damaging in the early stages of trading.

Most novices never get past their first few trades because they lose a lot of money even before they come to recognise that trading is not easy. One of the biggest difficulties in trading is to organise all the information available in a way that fits in with everything else. I will divulge what I call the Trading Methodology

Development Process, which shows you how you can develop your own trading methodology.

I will begin discussing the two approaches you may choose to analyse the markets: fundamental and technical analysis. I will discuss the pros and the cons of both and I will tell you which one I have chosen for myself and why.

I will then show you how you can read charts because if you cannot read charts, it would be like trading blind. I will set out examples to get you to start thinking in terms of charts and graphs. I will show you how to identify both short-term and long-term trends. By the end of this section, you will be able to analyse the markets using classical charting techniques used by traders before computers came about. You can learn to know when the market is likely to change trends or breakout from confined trading channels.

I will then introduce you to the most vital tools you need to analyse the markets. These tools are called 'indicators'. They are the building blocks of what is going to become your trading strategy. You will be able to understand the advantages and disadvantages of each of the 'indicators' you learn.

In the chapter after that, I will give you a thorough presentation of the components of a trading system. I will go on to introduce a few more ways of entering and exiting the market. We will then put all these components in a system. You will eventually be able to test a system and assess its strengths and its weaknesses. Your trading system is going to be your 'weapon' as you engage the market.

Having created a 'weapon', you need the armour of risk-management to protect yourself from the non-stop attack the market can inflict on your account. This armour is that of position-sizing, which impacts on your risk-management and money management. I will use all three terms interchangeably. I will reveal the key to what kept me from detrimental losses and the reasoning why it works. You need to know how to manage your risk so your money will last for as long as it possibly can.

Research shows the key to succeeding in trading is to survive long enough to have the time to learn about yourself and the market. If you lose all your money, you get kicked out of the market. The game is over.

Most traders have problems following their plans. In one of the later chapters, I will take you through the psychological issues that all traders come to deal with when they begin trading the markets with their trading systems. We will look at ways to minimise the impact your psychology may have on your trading. This will help pinpoint what you need to do to improve.

CHAPTER 6: PREPARATION

Most people who begin trading, fail dismally because they have prepared themselves inadequately. They enter the market not knowing that some preparation is essential. The process seems simple: buy a bunch of shares or currencies, wait for their value to go up and when it does, sell them at a profit. Then, you do it again.

Trading is deceptively easy and this is what lures most people to the markets. Armed with their hopes to make tons of money, they enter the markets with the expectations of making all of their dreams come true. However, people come out of the markets in shock and confusion after having lost most of the funds they have worked so hard for.

The markets are where some of the brightest and most talented people in the world come to play. Trading is the name of their game and their objective is simple: take money from other people who have come to the market to 'steal' theirs. That may be an obtuse remark; however, it needs to be put as such to anybody considering entering the markets. It is important to recognise the nature of trading for what it is. With total financial disaster being a possibility, the danger to a person entering the market unprepared is just as dreadful as it is when a person goes to war equipped with nothing more than a water pistol.

HOW CAN A TRADER PREPARE?

Traders can prepare themselves by doing the following:
a) Getting educated to gain the knowledge of the methods, tools, skills and the mindset necessary to trade effectively;
b) Preparing their minds to allow them to learn new behaviour and new thinking patterns in a manner that would be conducive to trading and
c) Preparing their finances so they can be in a position to trade, with money that they can afford to lose.

GETTING EDUCATED

A novice trader needs to educate himself about every aspect of trading. This includes getting to know the different methods to conduct analysis, build trading strategies, manage risks and overcome potential psychological barriers that affect trading behaviour. By researching these tools, a trader will become aware of what the future may hold so he can start preparing for the later stages of his development.

A novice trader can educate himself or herself by reading books. The chance to read a book written by someone who has traded the market is the closest you can get to the mind, the philosophy and the methods of an experienced trader. They are amazing because the lessons the author has taken years to learn are compressed into several pages that are tiny in comparison to the wisdom and experience they contain. Read as much as you can from many different sources. This is one of the few means that can give you the knowledge needed for trading. For those who find it hard to learn from books, see if there are any trustworthy seminars or lectures conducted on the topic.

PREPARING THE MIND

To prepare the mind for trading means to identify any set of limiting beliefs a trader has, which may hinder his or her ability to learn and develop. Only by doing this may the trader become free to learn new patterns of thinking and a new set of behaviours that would help him achieve his goal.

The following human traits and characteristics stifle the ability of a person to succeed in trading:
- a) Being lazy to do what it takes;
- b) Having too much pride to admit when you are wrong;
- c) Being fearful about the market;
- d) Being envious of other people's successes and
- e) Being greedy and nothing is ever enough.

Below, are beliefs that people may have about trading that make it difficult for them to trade:
- a) Trading is easy,
- b) Trading is hard,
- c) Trading is dangerous,
- d) Trading is about the money,
- e) Trading is fun and exciting,
- f) Trading is for men only and
- g) Trading is a useless profession.

People also hinder their trading performances because of the following beliefs they may have about themselves:
- a) They do not have the right 'brains' for trading;
- b) They need to get a 'real job' and
- c) They do not deserve success.

THE CONSEQUENCES OF PSYCHOLOGICAL QUALITIES THAT GET IN THE WAY OF TRADING

Sloth (Laziness)

The likely result of being lazy is that individuals fail to take the opportunity to learn about all the necessary methods, skills and techniques. Laziness leads to traders relying on other people and events outside themselves to bring them success. Instead of doing what they need to do, some people would prefer to gossip, look for stock tips, rely solely on the advice of their brokers or fund managers and buy magical software that claims to know it all. When none of these short-cuts work, they blame their failures on a computer program, an event or another person. It could be anything or anybody but never themselves. By delaying everything they need to do, novice traders are essentially wasting their time.

Pride

By having too much pride in admitting that they are wrong, some novice traders forget that the market does not care about their opinion. The market goes up or down regardless of what the trader thinks or does. The sooner he realises this, the quicker it is for him to progress.

Fear

After a series of losses, novice traders will begin to fear the market and begin drawing conclusions that may include the market being unpredictable, mysterious or uncontrollable. These fears stop the novice trader from doing what they need to do. They risk misdiagnosing the sources of their trading blunders. For example, a trader is fearful not because the market is malicious. It is because somewhere deep inside; the trader has a lot of self-doubt. He has little confidence because he did not research, develop and test a trading system as well as he should have, before using it.

Envy

By comparing themselves to other people and by being envious of what others have, some traders will create unnecessary pressure and conflict within themselves and with those people they may feel envious of. This can lead to an individual justifying what he has done in the past or he may put other people down just because he perceives them to have more than he has. Being envious of other people is a waste of time and effort. It will simply muddle the focus and concentration needed for the real task.

Greed

Greed is experienced when the rewards received are never enough. Greed interferes when the market is showing signs of reversing and the trader still does not close his trade at a profit because he wants more. The market does not care about the needs of any petty individual. It does not care that a trader needs more money to pay for the bills or if he is trying to make up for the losses of last month. As a trader, be happy with whatever the market gives you. If it begins to show signs that it is about to take back your open profits, and this confirms your analysis, then do not hesitate to take your profits while they are still there.

THE CONSEQUENCES OF PEOPLE'S BELIEFS ABOUT THE NATURE OF TRADING

The beliefs that trading is easy, hard, exciting, boring and useless are not necessarily false; however, a trader needs to identify which belief is most influential to his decisions because each one has its own set of complications.

The Danger In Believing That Trading Is Easy

The danger in believing that trading is easy is the lack of readiness. This belief can lead people to be unaware of the risks of trading and as a result, they do little research. As a result, their minds are poorly prepared for all the psychological assault that people inflict on themselves when they trade.

The Dangers In Believing That Trading Is Hard

The dangers in believing that trading is hard are that of discouragement and fear. If a person believes that trading is hard, then this may cause him to be discouraged about his own prospect for success in his endeavour. This may result in traders admitting defeat too early and give up their efforts before they have even begun. They may be denying themselves the opportunity to take on what could be the most suited profession for them. Trading may be hard, but so is any enterprise.

The Risk Of Believing That Trading Is Dangerous

Every business has its own set of risks but there are ways of mitigating the results of these risks. A person who believes that trading is dangerous may avoid it altogether. For this reason, he may remain ignorant for the rest of his life of an endeavour that might have been most suitable for him to excel in. Donald Trump and Robert Kiyosaki have both written in their books that: it is the individual that makes any form of investment dangerous. If you can trust yourself to do what you need to do to make sure that you are not exposing yourself to unnecessary and uncalculated risks, then trading is no more dangerous for you than any other business venture.

The Danger In Believing That Trading Is About Gaining A Lot Of Money

In the beginning, the focus in trading should not entirely be on making money…not until there are signs of consistent growth and improvement. Focusing on how much money he can make, encourages the individual to exercise risky trading behaviour. The prime directive for a novice trader should be to preserve his capital. If the novice is able to hang on to his money at the end of his first trading year, he would be doing well in comparison to many other individuals who will have already 'washed-out' of the markets.

The Risk Of Believing That Trading Is For Men Only

Women who believe this, risk losing out on the opportunity to do something that they might love and be good at. It is common for society to classify men and women simplistically. There are physiological and psychological differences between the sexes, but it does not mean that one is more suited to trade than the other.

Women are generally more emotional and this does not necessarily mean that it is bad for trading. It may cause them to associate more pain to losing; therefore, they will avoid taking big risks at the beginning of their careers. Men are generally not like this. They think they are measured by how much losses they can take. They keep holding on to ever-increasing losses, to the detriment of their trading accounts.

Personally, I do not believe that the success of a trader has anything to do with gender. It is up to individuals to understand their behaviour so they can identify which of their characteristics work for them and which ones don't. An individual needs to know when, and in which circumstances they thrive, so they can find a way to capitalise on their advantages. They also need to recognise when, and in which circumstances they become vulnerable, so they can find a way to mitigate the effects of their weaknesses.

The Danger In Believing That Trading Is Fun And Exciting

The danger in operating primarily under this belief is that of addiction. Trading can create an excitement that people can become addicted to, resembling the emotions experienced by people addicted to gambling. This belief about trading can drive the wrong individuals to the market: individuals who may be psychologically ill-suited for trading.

The Danger In Believing That Trading Is A Useless Profession

Trading adds liquidity to the market. Liquidity increases the efficiency of the market to ensure that buyers are not paying more than they need to and sellers are getting the best possible price for their commodities. The belief that trading is a useless profession just because it does not produce a product or render a service, harms the trader's performance because it creates a conflict within the individual. This conflict will cause the trader to unconsciously sabotage his or her success. This belief is connected with an individual's definition of what a 'real job' should be. Individuals who have this sentiment run the risk of suffering from the belief that they are also unworthy or undeserving of any trading rewards.

THE CONSEQUENCES OF LIMITING BELIEFS

(Please note that the comments below do not substitute the advice of a qualified therapist.)

People hinder their performance because of the limiting beliefs they may have about themselves. These beliefs come from the psychological issues that traders have trouble integrating. The conflict exists between what an individual wants to believe versus what he believes. The former dictates what he wants to be doing, the latter dictates what he is actually doing.

The Belief Of Not Having The 'Brains' For Trading

Some people believe that trading is only a game for the highly intellectual. There are many concepts from different topics that a trader needs to cover and there are skills that may take a long time to develop. However, brainpower is not everything. It is not true in the real world and it is not true in trading. Many people who have become successful in our society are not necessarily the people with the highest intellect. In fact, most of them say that their key to success had been to employ people who are a lot smarter than they are. Studies of trading accounts have shown that success in the intellectual professions does not guarantee an individual's success in trading.

Victor Sperandeo is a top trader in Wall Street. In his interview with Jack D. Schwager[31], he said that to be a successful trader, you need to be able to admit your mistakes. Generally, 'smart' people are so used to being 'correct' all the time and to their detriment, it makes it difficult to admit that they are wrong even when the market is against them.

The Dangers Of Having A Limited Concept Of What A 'Real Job' Is

A trader may have to take up a part-time or a full-time job to cover living expenses and other needs. But to give up on trading based purely on one's notion of what a 'real job' is supposed to be, may be a limiting belief. Many successful actors, musicians, sports people, entrepreneurs, inventors, scientists and leaders would have never reached their current status, had they listened to the people who ridiculed their chosen career paths.

The Dangers Of Feeling 'Unworthy' Of Success

For one reason or another, some traders instinctively believe that they do not deserve to be successful. If a trader decides to trade, it is important to confront this issue before trading with real money. The market could be an expensive place for an individual to try to resolve any existing self-doubts.

THE ONGOING NEED TO BE AWARE OF YOUR PSYCHOLOGY

If you are a novice trader, you will experience anxiousness. This is because psychologically, you have to deal with the constant

---

[31] Jack D. Schwager, *The New Market Wizards* (1992), p266.

possibility that you can make money beyond your wildest dreams while you risk losing money that you have worked so hard for. You are never sure if you are conducting your business 'right'. This is a natural part of your progression as a trader. There is no short-cut around this. The only way to get comfortable with the market is by continuously engaging in it. Do become more aware of how you think and how you react to different market conditions. You will eventually come to understand your behaviour and be able to pinpoint areas where you need to improve.

PREPARING YOUR FINANCES

People need to think clearly when they are in the market. It is the desperate need for money that brings ruin to many people because it rushes them to do something without properly assessing the risks. Before engaging the market, a trader needs to make sure he separates his need for money from his trading. Below is a list of suggestions, reminders and tips that may help in achieving this.

KEEP A FULL-TIME OR A PART-TIME JOB

The title of this book does not suggest that trading is so easy that anybody can do it part-time. It is to the contrary. Unless there is a reserve of funds that can last for about a year or two, a trader will need to continue working to ensure he covers the ongoing costs of living.

There are times when a trader makes more in one day from trading than the amount he gets paid in a month's wages. When this happens, the biggest and most common mistake for an inexperienced trader to do is to quit his job. It is recommended that a trader holds back the temptation to hand in his resignation until there are signs of consistent growth in his account month after month.

Apart from the difficulty of attaining success from trading, there are also other factors that a person needs to consider before he decides to trade for a living, because trading has its own challenges.

Firstly, it is a solitary endeavour. This could pose a problem for individuals who are social by nature. Secondly, if an individual has a history of lacking time management and self-management skills, he might need the existence of established processes, structures and rules to work conscientiously. Thirdly, there is no safety net of sick leaves or annual leaves. If something happens that affects the ability of a person to analyse and carry out trades, no money will be deposited in the bank account.

UNDERCAPITALISATION

The Challenges Of Having A Small Account

A trader needs to have a decent-size trading account since one of the main causes for failure identified by prior studies has been that of undercapitalisation. There needs to be enough money in a trading account to sustain the costs of trading. These costs include data costs and commission fees and other transaction costs. There are also education costs involved including the costs of books, seminars, trade magazines and such.

There is one factor that has a significant effect on the longevity of a trading account: the minimum contract size allowed by a broker. Contract size is the size of a trade. If you buy 200 shares or 100,000 US Dollars, the size of your contract is 200 shares or in the latter case, 100,000 US Dollars. A bigger position means a bigger loss if the trade goes against the trader. If the broker requires a minimum contract size that is too big in relation to the size of a trader's account, there is a high likelihood that a small series of losing trades can wipe out the account.

Therefore, you need to allocate as much funds as you comfortably can when you open your trading account and choose a broker that provides you with a minimum contract size.

The Advantages Of Having A Small Account

A novice trader should be excited about the advantages of being undercapitalised. A novice trader having access to a big account is like a little kid running and playing around with a big knife or like a drunk driver driving around with a big truck. He has the potential and the capacity to injure himself and others.

In the beginning, a trader is going to make many mistakes. Every time that happens, he will incur a loss. He has no choice. If he wants to learn how to trade, he has to expect to make mistakes. The losses he incurs are the costs of his training and his education. Having a small account has its advantages because of this. A novice with a small account will be forced to open small trades. In dollar terms, his losses are little compared with the losses of a person who is trading more than a hundred-thousand-dollar account. In other words, his education will cost less if he has a small account.

TRADE WITH MONEY YOU CAN AFFORD TO LOSE

It is important that an individual commits only a small part of his total cash funds to trading. The consequences are too great to be risking more capital than you can afford to lose. It is important to accept that risk completely. It is not enough for a trader to say, 'yes, I can afford to lose this money', but instinctively only accepting one possibility: the possibility that the money will grow. A novice trader must prepare for the likelihood that he or she may never see his or her money again.

DO NOT BORROW MONEY TO TRADE

Master traders get paid a lot by growing other people's money, but most people reading this book are not master traders just yet. Borrowing money or trading other people's money adds extra apprehension that you do not need to deal with in the early days of your trading. It is hard to focus on learning when investors are constantly hounding you about your performance as well as creditors threatening to pull out their money during inopportune times. Until you develop the skills, the strategies and the mindset to be a profitable trader, your focus should be on growing your account regardless of how small it may be. When you become a good trader, people will eventually want to invest big money in your business. Until then, you cannot afford to take in 'nervous' investors.

Before most people even come to recognise the errors they may have made in their assumptions and the mistakes they may have made in their judgment, it would already be too late. They have already lost enough. By then, most people would be hurting financially, emotionally and psychologically. Traders can save themselves much of this pain if they understand the need to educate themselves, to prepare their minds, to prepare their finances and to have reasonable expectations about trading before engaging the market. This will ensure that they can progress to the next stage.

CHAPTER 7: THE TRADING METHODOLOGY DEVELOPMENT PROCESS

Traders who survive their early years are then faced with the challenge of having to deal with a vast amount of information that they need to absorb to become proficient. Individuals will come upon a plethora of ideas from many disciplines including finance, business, economics, mathematics, science, art and psychology, all of which are relevant and useful to trading.

In this lies another reason why trading is hard to master. A trader accumulates too much information for him to piece it together in a coherent and logical manner. There are so many aspects to consider and there are too many methods and approaches out there to include them all.

We, as a society, have created structures for individuals to follow. Before I began trading, life had structure for me. I went to primary school so I could go to high school. I had to choose my subjects in high school so I could specialise in university. Finally, after collecting my degree, the next step was to get a job. There were logical steps for me to follow.

When individuals enter the world of trading, there are no rules, no structures and no guidelines. There is no authority and nobody is qualified to tell them what to do with their own money. It is up to them to find a way to stop losing and unless they have a close relative who is a successful trader, their only hope in learning how to trade is by reading books.

I have come across books by traders who wrote about their trading rules, how they disciplined their minds and controlled their emotions to be in sync with the market. Most books had their own specific focus: technical indicators, psychology, developing trading systems, etc…while others spoke of different approaches. They had been great books to read. However, what I was looking for was a process, a flow chart that showed a novice trader like me, what I needed to do right from the beginning.

What I will share with you next is the process of how to develop your own trading method based on my entire trading methodology. A trading methodology is a guideline of how beginners may go about starting their own trading business, incorporating indicators, trading systems and risk management strategies. Equipped with this formula, novice traders will speed up their learning a lot faster than I did.

THE TRADING METHODOLOGY DEVELOPMENT PROCESS

1. Choose Your Trading Style – Your Approach To Analysing The Market

The first step in developing your trading methodology is to choose the analytical approach you are going to use. There are predominantly two types to choose from: fundamental analysis and technical analysis. (*See chapter 8.*)

2. Devise A Trading System

After you have chosen your approach, you need to devise a trading system based on that analysis. A trading system is simply a set of rules which helps you decide how you are going to open and close your trades. (*See chapter 12.*)

Your Trading System Will Be Based On Your Tools And Your Indicators

You need to create your trading system based on the tools and indicators of your chosen analytical approach. Technical analysis uses mathematical calculations based on price and transaction volumes, while fundamental analysis uses indicators that measure specific aspects of a company or an economy. If you are trading shares, then you need to look at indicators about the company you have invested in. If you are trading currencies, you need to look at the economy of the country you have invested in. I touch on fundamental analysis in this book; however, if you choose to use the fundamental approach to analyse the market, other books would probably be more relevant to you. However, it might be worth your time to see if there are ideas here that you can use because regardless of what analytical approach you choose, I believe the subsequent steps are still relevant to any form of trading. (*See chapter 11.*)

Are The Rules Going To Be Discretionary Or Mechanical?

The set of rules that make up your entire trading system can be discretionary or mechanical. Mechanical trading systems comprise of rigid rules that a trader must simply follow like a robot follows a command. Proper execution of such trading systems does not tolerate any deviation. Discretionary trading systems on the other hand, are made up of rather 'loose' rules which traders may choose to interpret at their own 'discretion'. This means that their analysis, intellect and emotions play a major role in their trading decisions. (*See chapter 12.*)

3. Test Your Trading System

After devising a trading system, you will need to test its

validity. If most of your theories and assumptions are correct, then you owe it to yourself to see if your system would have made money in the past. Past performance never guarantees future performance, but if your system could not have survived the previous periods, then what indications would you have that it will survive the future? (*See chapter 13.*)

4. Devise A Position-Sizing Strategy To Protect Your Money

You need to consider the size of your positions and your trades. Good position-sizing strategies protect your trading account from being wiped out by a series of losses. At the same time it ensures that you are taking position sizes that are big enough to maximise the growth of your trading account. (*See chapter 14.*)

5. Test Your Trading System Combined With Your Risk-Management Strategy

You then need to test your trading system and see how it performs when you combine it with your risk-management strategy.

6. Make An Early Evaluation If It Is Likely That Your Psychological Profile Can Withstand The Trading System And Your Risk-Management Strategy

At this stage, you need to make an initial assessment whether you are psychologically fitted to carry out the trading strategy you have created for yourself. There is no use having a great trading system with a suited money management strategy if you cannot follow your own rules.

You need to work on your trading rules, your position-sizing strategy and your psychology at the same time because they are all interconnected. They affect one another. Changing one affects the other two. Collectively, it is how these three perform together that will dictate how well you will perform as a trader. If at any point, you need to revise your rules, then do so before you move on to the next step.

7. Execute Your System

Based on the research and the testing you have done, you should be able to assess whether you have a trading system that might succeed. If so, start trading it so you can test it in real-life. Watch how your trading system engages the market. Observe your behaviour to see if you are psychologically fit for the system. I will be discussing the topic of discipline and psychology in Chapter 15.

8. Re-Evaluate Your System

You need to re-evaluate your system as soon as you realise that you made incorrect assumptions about the nature of the market or yourself. If you have made an error in judgment regarding a variable in your trading system or in your money management strategy, then you need to get back to those variables and make some changes. If there are changes you need to make about your system, then go back to step 3 and run the process from there. After that, take your system and position-sizing strategy for a 'test-drive' again. Trade the adjusted system and see how it behaves in the market and if you can consistently follow your rules without breaking them. Continue this process until your trading account shows signs of consistent growth. This could take you a long time. Many traders get stuck here. So be patient. As soon as there is proof that your trading account makes a steady climb month after month, then congratulate yourself for having achieved what few are able to do.

9. Optimise Your System

The market is never the same. It is forever-changing. If your system worked last year, there is no guarantee that it will work this year. So if you had been fortunate enough to devise a profitable trading system that has worked in the past, you need to continue adapting your trading methodology to the never-ending transformation of the market to ensure that you stay profitable.

THE TRADING METHODOLOGY DEVELOPMENT PROCESS FLOW CHART

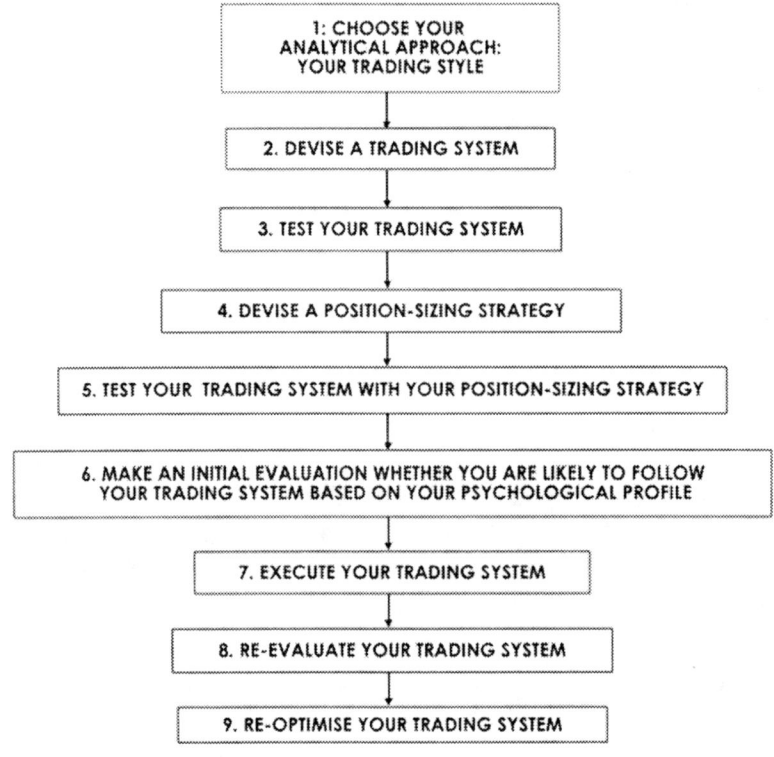

Image 3: The Trading Methodology Development Process Flow Chart

The diagram above is a visual summary of the process you can follow to develop your own methodology in trading, whatever market you want to trade. Each chapter after this either complements or goes deeper into the concepts implicated by this process.

CHAPTER 8: ANALYSING THE MARKET: FUNDAMENTAL VS TECHNICAL ANALYSIS

You need to analyse the market in some way before you can extract money from it. Your trading style is simply the approach you take on how you would like to analyse the market. Therefore, the first step you need to do to develop your own trading methodology is to decide what your trading style is going to be.

There are predominantly two approaches when it comes to analysing markets. You can approach it using fundamental analysis or you can approach it using technical analysis. People have made great fortunes regardless of whether they used technical or fundamental analysis. If either works for you and it makes sense, then use it. If you have been analysing the markets with one method, you can try the other. I have read of traders who, for years, have been unsuccessful in using one approach and only after trying the other approach, did they find success.

Before I bring your attention to these two major styles, please note there are other approaches which people choose to analyse the markets. For example, some traders are applying ideas gained from the study of artificial intelligence and neural networking. Others also use more unusual approaches like astrology. I choose not to discuss them here because I do not know much about them to give you a better understanding of how they work.

FUNDAMENTAL ANALYSIS

In one word, the focus of fundamental analysis is: value. Traders using fundamental analysis focus on finding out whether the currency is overvalued or undervalued relative to other currencies. They work hard in trying to estimate what the 'intrinsic' value of a currency will be or should be. They base their estimates on the different factors that impact on the demand and supply for a currency. They will compare this theoretical value to that of the current value of the currency. If the market value of the currency is below its 'intrinsic' value, then they will buy the currency. If the market value of a currency is above its 'intrinsic value' then, they will sell the currency.

Fundamental analysts build conceptual models that emulate the financial and economic realities of the world to guess what the 'intrinsic value' of a currency is. They mainly look towards macroeconomic indicators which are released periodically by various government and academic sources. They work with social theories and economic formulas to anticipate what the market is likely to do next.

Two of the most important indicators for currency traders are interest rates and international trade, including all factors affecting an economy's imports, exports and productivity. They also look at the following indicators:

a) The Gross Domestic Product (GDP), which is a measure of the value of economic production of a country;
b) M2 Money Supply, which measures the total amount of all currencies;
c) The Consumer Price Index (CPI), which is a measure of the cost of living and
d) The Producer Price Index (PPI), which is a measurement of the cost of producing goods and retail sales.

Interest rates affect the value of a particular currency because it is the rate of return for those investors who invest their money in that country. That is why high interest rates attract foreign investors to an economy. This is believed to strengthen the economy's currency and if the effect is strong enough, the value of the currency will appreciate.

For stock market investors, however, the increase in the interest rate increases the cost of borrowing. If the cost of borrowing increases, then companies will borrow less money. The operations which require borrowed money are held back. This hinders the operations of companies. This decline in operations is perceived to have a negative effect on the company's profitability. This will then prompt investors to sell their share holdings. Reduced profits turn investors away. If foreign investors are turned away, then the demand for the local currency will reduce. A cut in the demand for the currency applies a downward pressure on that currency. This may cause it to depreciate relative to the value of another currency.

Therefore, on the one hand, higher interest rates have an effect of strengthening a currency; while on the other hand, they have the effect of weakening it. It is up to you, as an analyst and a trader, to work out what the net effect would be.

In using fundamental analysis to determine the theoretical value of a currency, you also need to take a look at the country's levels of import and export. Imports cause money to flow out of the country to buy foreign-made goods. Exports bring in money from foreign consumers who need to buy the local currency in exchange for theirs, before being able to buy local goods and services. In a case where there are more imports than exports, the country is said to have a deficit international trade balance. Where exports are greater than imports, there is a surplus.

An economy much prefers to have more exports than it has imports. This would have the net effect of strengthening its currency because the foreign demand for domestic goods and services increases the demand for the domestic currency. This will then add an upward pressure for the currency to appreciate in value.

As a fundamental analyst you would also need to look at the country's leaders and their stance on important political, economic and socio-cultural issues. This is because the actions and the decisions that these leaders make, have a major impact on future events and decisions. All of these factors affect the value of the domestic currency.

From my observation, even though most people do not fully understand the explanation behind most of the generally-accepted models and principles of macroeconomics, they have a tendency to believe that the only way to profit from the currency market is to consider all the financial, political and socio-cultural landscapes of an economy.

The complexity of using fundamental analysis to trade currencies is a barrier for most people. Even highly-educated analysts who are familiar with the valuation concepts that we as a society have come up with, still disagree with one another when asked about what they think the real value of a currency should be. The calculation of 'true' value is the main reason an investor would use this approach in analysing the markets. Since this is the case, it is disconcerting that highly-competent experts disagree on what the 'true' value of a tradable commodity should be.

It is not because fundamental analysis is hard that you should not use it. If you find it easy to grasp macroeconomic and valuation concepts, then perhaps fundamental analysis is the right style for you. There are several elite individuals, like George Soros, who have made tons of money with their innate ability to develop valuation models to accomplish their phenomenal feats.

TECHNICAL ANALYSIS

In one word, the main focus of technical analysis is: price. The underlying premise for technical analysis is: price discounts everything. There is no need to worry about what the theoretical or 'intrinsic' value of a commodity is because its current price considers everything that motivates buyers and sellers. It reflects all their fears, hopes, needs, resources and everything else from all that is known and understood to all that is not.

Technical analysis divides people into two major groups – the bulls and the bears. 'Bulls' are the people who act on the belief that the price will go up. 'Bears' are the people who act on the belief that the price will go down. The bulls push the market prices up with their 'horns' and the bears 'slash' the market prices down with their 'paws'.

Technical analysis helps the trader find out which of the two groups of people are stronger in their convictions. The stronger group will drive the direction of the market. This is why technical analysts focus on the price and its movements. It tells them who among the two groups are dominating. They plot this information on charts and graphs and study them. They run mathematical calculations based on these movements and create technical indicators that measure these movements in a way that is easy to interpret visually.

UNDERSTANDING THE SIGNIFICANCE OF PRICE

Why is price so important for technical analysts? To answer this question, we must first recognise that the market is made up of millions of people transacting. To get an even better understanding of the market, we narrow our focus on the market's most basic elements: two parties agreeing to conduct a transaction at an agreed price.

Consider a deal between two people where the price of a commodity increases. It is important for us to understand the reasons for, and the implications of, this price increase.

A buyer agrees to buy at a higher price only because he believes the higher price will still be lower than the price he can sell it for in the future[32]. If he hesitates, another buyer might come in and snatch the deal away from him. Therefore, he agrees to buy at a higher price because he fears missing out on a 'good' deal. He is the most eager buyer because he is the person who is willing to offer the most for that particular commodity.

The most eager seller on the other hand, is selling the commodity because he thinks the price of the instrument is going to go down. In comparison to all the other sellers, this person is the most eager person to sell his commodity at the lowest price.

We have two individuals: one is the most optimistic person in the market and the other is the most pessimistic person in the market at that particular time. Each hold opposite views about

---

[32] We are assuming a person who would trade because he wants to profit.

where the market is going. What happens when they make a decision is important. The buying pressure overpowers the selling pressure. This means that the buyers are more desperate for the commodity. Both then agree to transact at a higher price, which is going to be the new market price of the commodity.

The buyer and the seller are also the most willing and able to take action on their beliefs. To be in a position to conduct the transaction at that particular time, they would have had to overcome many factors – mentally, physically and emotionally. Despite the doubts and fears they might have held about the transaction, they still decided to go ahead with the deal.

What this implies to me is that: a commodity has no other theoretical or intrinsic value that is different to its market price because everything that should have, could have, or would have an impact on the market, has already done so. Therefore, price factors in everything there is to know and understand about the motivations of the buyers and the sellers. It also factors in everything else that we do not yet understand about what drives the market.

WHY I USE TECHNICAL ANALYSIS

If you have a feeling that technical analysis may be for you then read the reasons why I use it. I will run you through what I perceive to be the benefits of technical analysis over fundamental analysis. If my reasons make sense to you, then try using technical analysis as your approach in analysing the markets.

I use technical analysis to trade forex because of the following reasons:

1. It allows me to study the present behaviour of the market;
2. It allows me to study the past behaviour of the market;
3. Fundamental analysis does not take into account all factors affecting the market behaviour;
4. I would rather focus on what is happening instead of what should be happening;

5. Fundamental analysis is an important tool for firm analysts but not necessarily for private traders;
6. Technical analysis is a viable means for a private trader;
7. Technical trading systems are easier to test, assess and validate than fundamental trading systems;
8. I believe that fundamental analysis is for long-term trades;
9. I believe that fundamental analysis is useful in other markets but in forex, technical analysis quickens my decision process and
10. I can apply everything I learn from one market or one trading instrument to another.

1. It Allows Me To Study The Present Behaviour Of Market Participants

Charts are like opinion polls. They are a consensus of value of all the participants in the market. For every tick it goes up it means there had been a vote by two parties – the buyer and the seller – that the price should be going up. Both parties take action on their beliefs so, they transact at a higher price. Alternatively, for every tick it goes down, it is an agreement between two parties that the price is going to go down. Since the two parties act on this belief, they agree to transact at a lower price. To that effect, charts plot the collective behaviour of masses of people as time goes by. It goes up when most participants are feeling optimistic about the commodity. It goes down if most are feeling pessimistic about it.

2. It Allows Me To Study The Past Behaviour Of The Market

Charts give technical analysts an idea of the behaviour of all the traders, investors and other market participants in its history. The price chart provides an analyst an idea of how sensitive the price had been in relation to the events of the past. These events may include economic booms, wars, depressions and recessions. An analyst may then run tests to collect statistics on price data. This will help him recognise when the market is behaving normally or when it is not. Further, an analyst might notice that every time an event happens, another event follows 70% of the time and perhaps even find out that a third event may happen 60% of the time. After having identified such a relationship with some statistical certainty, then the trader needs to design a system that will capitalise on that 'edge'.

3. Fundamental Analysis Does Not Consider All Factors Affecting Market Behaviour

Fundamental analysis works with economic models and theories. It assumes that people buy and sell similarly in the 'rational' manner assumed by these theoretical representations of the real world. In reality however, people do not always behave in a manner that is as 'rational' as these theories and formulas assume them to be. These models cannot incorporate everything in the real world that can impact on the price.

Firstly, psychology impacts on the price. Just because a company is anticipated to be more profitable in the future, it does not mean that people will buy its shares. They may know that they should be buying but they do not necessarily act on this knowledge. They may not buy because they may not have the money, or because they fear being wrong about their analysis regardless of how strongly they feel about it.

In addition, even if they are willing and able to buy, most people do not sit down to grab all the news articles and download all the economic indicators to calculate the price at which they should be buying or selling. Most market participants do not even know what these models are or how they can be used to calculate the intrinsic value of a share or a currency. They may get a stock tip from a friend or a relative who may have bought some shares that are now worth a little more. Many people would base their buying decision on this fact alone or on a rumour that it will go up in price. Would they even calculate the 'theoretical' share price? Not likely. What if the share price goes up higher than its theoretical value and is now considered to be overvalued? Most people would not know that. They would continue buying for as long as they are convinced by rumours that the price will go up some more. If you are 'bearish' in a 'bullish' market, you are going to lose money.

Secondly, fundamental analysis does not consider how other people may trade the markets. Many people use methods that deviate a lot from what fundamental analysts believe as being 'rational'. There are many people applying scientific and mathematical concepts from other branches of study to the way they trade the market. There are specialists out there using new methods based on neural networks and artificial intelligence. Other people might base their decisions on studying the stars and their formations, none of which have anything to do with the value of a company or an economy. Psychology and other methods of trading do have the potential to invalidate what fundamental analysts believe should happen.

4. I Would Rather Focus On What Is Happening Instead Of What 'Should' Be Happening

Continuing from the line of reasoning above, it just seems to me that fundamental analysis focuses on what 'should' be happening, not on what 'is' actually happening.

5. Fundamental Analysis Is Important For Fund Management Analysts But Not Necessarily For Private Traders

For a person making a living as an analyst, fundamental analysis is important because he can use logic to back up the recommendations he makes to his company's clients. As long as your recommendations are rational, then you are a good analyst. That is what you get paid to do. If you use technical analysis, most investors will not understand how a squiggly technical indicator has anything to do with the value of an investment. For a fund management business, you would want your analysts to use fundamental analysis, because it would make more sense to your clients when you explain the reasoning behind your investments. If a prediction turns out to be wrong, nobody can blame the fund management business or their analysts as long as their investment decisions were based on logic and thorough information. All mishaps can just be blamed on the 'irrationality' of the market.

If you are a trader, however, you can only make money if you go the same direction as the market. If you are in a 'long' position, you will never profit if the market keeps going down, even if your 'bullish' predictions are logical. As a trader or an investor, is it more important for you to make predictions and find supporting evidence to back up your theories? Or is it more important to try to be on the same direction as the market, regardless of whether it makes sense to you or not?

There is an ocean of difference between the motive of an analyst and a trader. An analyst gets paid by making sensible analysis. A trader gets rewarded only when he follows the direction of the market. For that reason, it is important for a person engaging the markets to 'dig deep' and find out if they are deciding like an analyst or if they are deciding like a trader.

6. Technical Analysis Is A Viable Tool For A Private Trader

There are big organisations that hire hundreds, even thousands of professionals, competent experts and analysts. They have the resources and the network of people that I, as an individual, may only dream of having. What does it matter if I thought the price of a commodity was going to go up? My opinion is only going to be one among the many…like a grain of sand on a beach. So, like a small fish competing for food in a big pond, a private trader has to think differently and use different strategies to create his own game.

Instead of trying to come up with my own opinion of what the value of a commodity should be, I just wait for everybody else to do their own calculations, make their own assessments and make a decision. The results of their decision – as well as the decisions of thousands of other market participants having different beliefs, methods and techniques – will all be reflected on the price chart. If the buying pressure is stronger, then the price will go up. If the sellers are more desperate, then the price will come down. All I have to do is pick the more dominant side because they are going to dictate where the price will go. If the market is flat, then I stay out since all the experts cannot agree on where they should 'drive' the market next.

If you are a private trader, trading at home, this reason could well be the deciding factor on why you would want to use technical analysis.

7. Technical Trading Systems Are Far Easier To Test, Assess And Validate Than Fundamental Trading Systems

When hard-earned money is on the line, a trader would want to know his or her chances for success. That is why testing a system is important. By testing my system on past data, it is easy to isolate the assumptions I make and test if they are valid or not. I will be able to get some form of statistical data that tells me what my chances of success are before I have confidence to trade that system. Most of the time there is no other way for fundamental analysts and theorists to test their ideas but to test them in the real world. Thus, it takes more time and money to prove or debunk a theory.

8. Fundamental Analysis Is For Long-Term Trades

I believe that fundamental analysis is useful only for long-term trades that are at least more than three months. I say three months because it would usually take that long to see the effects of any economic data after its release. If you don't plan to stay in a trade for more than three months, then perhaps you may be better off using technical analysis to analyse the markets. Please note that some fundamental analysts still say that anything less than three years is short term.

9. Fundamental Analysis Is Useful In Other Markets But In Forex, Technical Analysis Quickens My Decision Process

Fundamental analysis is useful for investors who acquire assets primarily for 'residual income'[33]. But in forex trading, you trade for capital gains so 'intrinsic value' becomes secondary to 'price'.

Fundamental analysis is also important in markets where fundamental factors impact greatly on the price of a commodity. If you are trading corn futures for example, the seasons impact on the price of corn contracts. In forex, currency values are impacted by too many factors for me to study. Thus, I find it simpler to observe the price which already takes everything into account.

10. I Can Apply Everything I Learn From One Market Or Commodity To Another

Technical analysis is a good approach because you can apply your knowledge, skill and proficiency to trade any market or commodity. With fundamental analysis, this is not the case. The knowledge you have of trading corn will be different to the knowledge that you will need to trade currencies, for example.

Conclusion

Whichever analytical approach you plan to use – fundamental or technical analysis – is of no consequence. Both schools of thought have been able to produce successful traders and investors. What matters is that you choose an approach that makes sense to you. If you choose to use fundamental analysis, I still believe the process of how to develop a trading methodology I outline in this book is important. Besides, fundamental analysts can and do use technical indicators as tools to confirm the validity of their theories and assumptions. This helps them with their entry and exit strategies.

---

[33] Sources of residual income include rent payments (for real-estate investors), dividend payments (for share investors) and interest payments (for money lenders).

CHAPTER 9: HOW TO 'READ' CHARTS

I am sure that whichever brokerage firm you choose to work with, you will get access to graphical charts that help you analyse the markets. If they do not provide these, look for another broker. Trading any market without looking at a chart, even if you are a fundamental analyst, is like trying to find your way around an unfamiliar terrain in the dark without a flashlight.

Technical analysis examines the price and uses indicators. Please note that share traders also analyse and apply technical indicators on volume. Option traders analyse open interests[34].

The first time you look at a chart, it might not make much sense to you. All you probably see, is a bunch of lines, strokes, rectangles, curves and more lines. As you will eventually discover, it is amazing how much information these seemingly, nonsensical blots of light on your computer screen do contain.

TIMEFRAME

When you look at a chart, you need to know the timeframe of the chart. Brokers typically provide charts with timeframes of 5 minutes, 30 minutes, 1 hour, 3 hours, 4 hours, 1 day or 1 week. Once you know the timeframe of price activity the chart is plotting, you know that each bar or candlestick represents the price action for that timeframe. If you are looking at hourly charts, then you

---

[34] Volume is the amount of shares transacted in a given period. Open Interest is the net long and short positions for any option contract.

know that every bar or candlestick is a representation of the movements of the price for each hour the market trades.

VIEWING PRICE DATA: LINES, BARS AND CANDLES

For every period that ticks over, a currency has its open price, its close price, its highest point and its lowest point during that particular period. In short, these prices are referred to as: open, close, high and low.

Close Lines

Plotting the close line is the simplest way to plot charts. Simply connect the closing price of each period. It ignores the opens, highs and lows. On the right of the chart below, you can see the closing price axis and the squiggly line shows what the closing price of the GBP/JPY has been between November 2004 and October 2005.

Image 4: Close Chart

Bar Charts

A bar chart displays the opens, highs, lows and closes with lines and dashes. Bar charts look like the ones shown below where: O = Open, H = High, L = Low and C = Close.

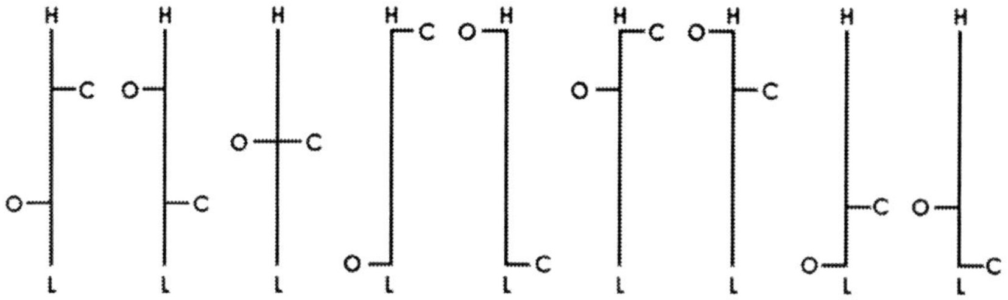

Image 5: HLOC Bars

The examples above are examples of HLOC (High-Low-Open-Close) Bars. Collectively, they can look like this:

Image 6: HLOC Bars – Group

Since forex is a 24-hour market, it has a continuous stream of price data broken up into the timeframe of the chart you are looking at. This means that usually, the closing of one bar automatically becomes the opening of another bar. This is why we sometimes ignore the opening prices when plotting forex charts. Some people plot H-L-C (High-Low-Close) bars instead of HLOC bars.

Japanese Candlesticks

A candlestick chart displays the opens, highs, lows and closes with candlestick-looking representations of price. Candlesticks look like the ones shown below where: O = Open, H = High, L = Low and C = Close.

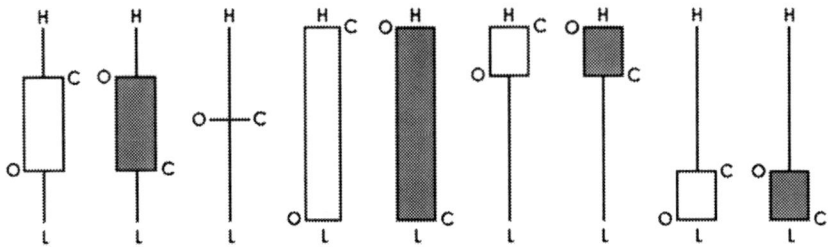

Image 7: Reading Japanese Candlesticks Individually

Collectively, candlesticks can look like this:

Image 8: Candlesticks – Group.

If you want to find out more about candlesticks, I refer you to Steve Nison's *Japanese Candlestick Charting Techniques*, published by the New York Institute of Finance, as well as *The Secret of Candlestick Charting* by Louise Bedford, published by Wrightbooks.

There are many books written about how to read bar-by-bar or candlestick-by-candlestick analysis. I am aware of them but I do not use them a lot and so I am not going to discuss them here.

The Range

The distance between the high price and the low price of a bar is called **the range**. You can improve your analysis of trends by considering the ranges of the bars or candlesticks.

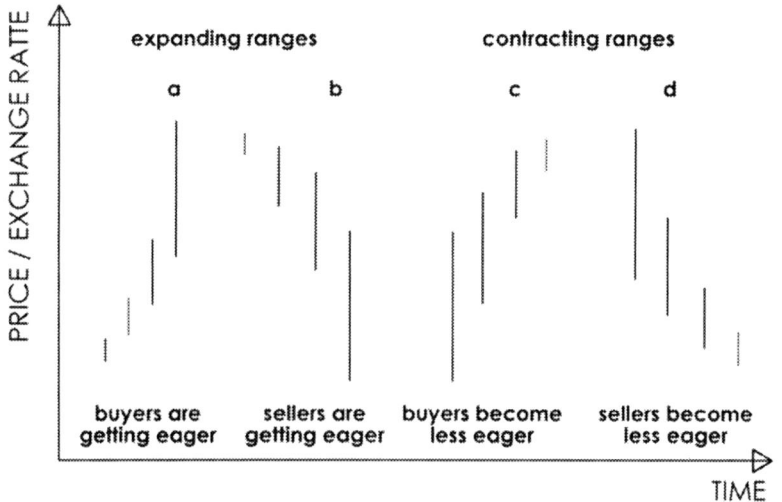

Image 9: Expanding & Contracting Ranges

a) When a few 'bulls' decide to buy, convinced that the price will go up and other people join in, the price accelerates upwards. As time goes by, the range of each bar becomes longer than the previous bar.

b) When a few 'bears' decide to sell, convinced that the price will go down and other people join the selling, the price will accelerate downwards as time goes on, the range expands.
c) When many 'bulls' decide to buy, convinced the price will go up but later these bulls reduce in number, the price slows down from its upward momentum and the range begins to contract as time goes by.
d) When many 'bears' decide to sell because they are convinced the price will go down but later, their number reduces. The price slows down its downward momentum and the range begins to contract as time goes by.

HOW TO BUY AND SELL CURRENCIES: 'LONG' OR 'SHORT' POSITIONS

Most people understand how they can profit if they buy at a low price initially and then sell at a higher price later, but not the other way around. Most people curl their eyebrows if you tell them you can make money by selling at a high price first before you can buy at a low price later. Unless you know how to use option instruments, you cannot do this with shares. However, when you are trading currency pairs, this is easy to do.

I will show you an example of what happens when you buy or sell a currency pair. This example is trading the USD/CAD, daily chart. Let's say that you are the trader. You take on trade A and trade B marked on the chart.

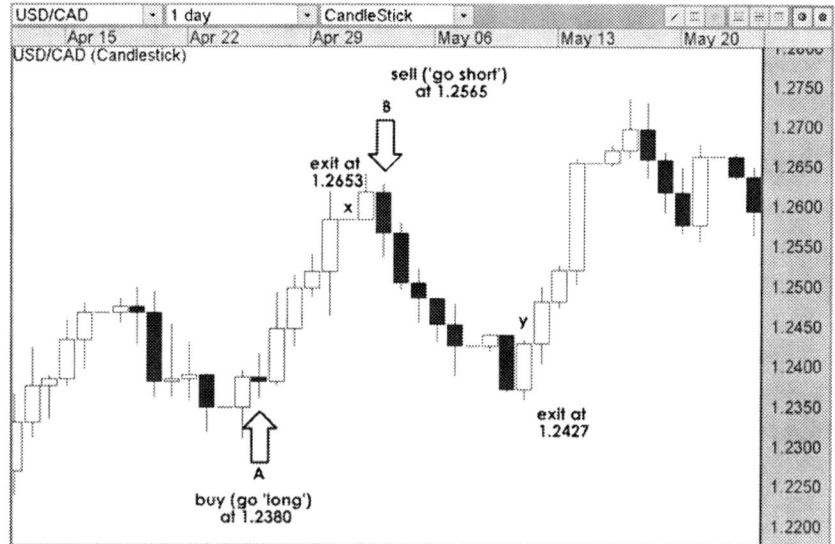

Image 10: Buying & Selling A Currency Pair

TRADE A

In this trade you want to buy or in other words, you take a 'long' position on the USD/CAD currency pair. Let's say your position size is 10,000 USDs.

a. You buy 10,000 USDs at an exchange rate of 1.2380 by 'short' selling 12,380 CADs.
b. You sell the 10,000 USDs and at an exchange rate of 1.2653 by buying 12,653 CADs.
c. You gain 273 CADs. If your trading account is in USDs, this gets converted into US Dollars and goes straight to your trading account at a value of 216 USDs.

After reading step (a), you were probably asking yourself how to buy 10,000 USDs when you do not have 12,380 CADs to sell. Note that you are 'short' selling 12,380 CADs. What this means is that you are effectively borrowing that money. We have discussed this in chapter 3 on 'trading on leverage' and 'margin lending'.

If you are trading on a margin of 200:1, you only need to put up a margin of 50 USDs[35] to gain 216 USDs. You do not lose

---

[35] $10,000 / 200 = $50

this $50, you get this margin back at the end of the trade. If the trade was a loser, you still get it back but your margin account will reduce by the amount of your loss.

WARNING:
Given this example, you may say that you have quadrupled your money in one transaction. The problem is that if the trade turned out to be a losing trade, and the market went the opposite direction, you would have lost $216 by putting up only $50! It is important that you understand the risks and the benefits of what it means to trade on a margin. **Leverage magnifies your gains but it also worsens your losses.**

TRADE B

In this trade you want to sell or in other words, take a 'short' position on the USD/CAD currency pair. Let's say your position size is 10,000 USDs.

- You 'short' sell 10,000 USDs at an exchange rate of 1.2565 and buy 12,565 CADs.
- You buy 10,000 USDs at an exchange rate of 1.2427 by selling 12,427 CADs.
- You gain 138 CADs. If your trading account is in USDs, these CADs convert into US Dollars and go straight into your trading account as 111 USDs[36].

UPWARD AND DOWNWARD TRADES OR POSITIONS

Remember from the last chapter that buying, selling, going 'long' and going 'short' are industry terms. To make it easier, I may refer to 'long' trades as 'upward trades' and 'short' trades as 'downward trades'.

---

[36] 138 * (1/1.2427) = 111

HOW TO IDENTIFY TRENDS

The Dow Theory is the combined work of Charles Dow, William Hamilton and Robert Rhea. They mainly studied equity markets but we can use technical analysis theories in any market and with any commodity. You can research more about this theory but I want to show you how it identifies a bull and a bear trend. The foundations that these three men have given us have become one of the cornerstone concepts in technical analysis today.

Short-Term Trends

The difference between the low and the high of a bar chart or a candlestick is **the range**. I will plot representations of the range below.

HOW TO IDENTIFY SHORT-TERM BULL TRENDS:

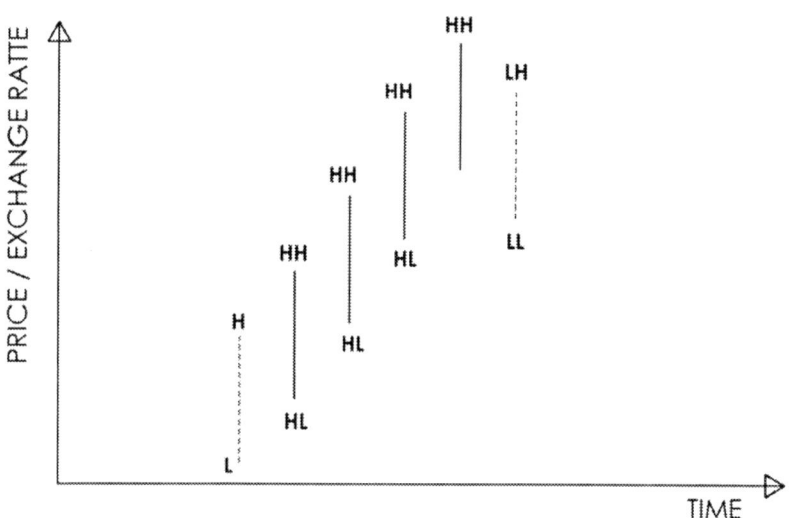

Image 11: Short-Term Bull Trends

Where: H – High, HH – Higher High, LH – Lower High, L – Low, LL –Lower Low, HL – Higher Low.

There is a bull trend when the price keeps making higher highs and higher lows. As soon as there is a lower low and a lower high, the bull trend has finished.

HOW TO IDENTIFY SHORT-TERM BEAR TRENDS:

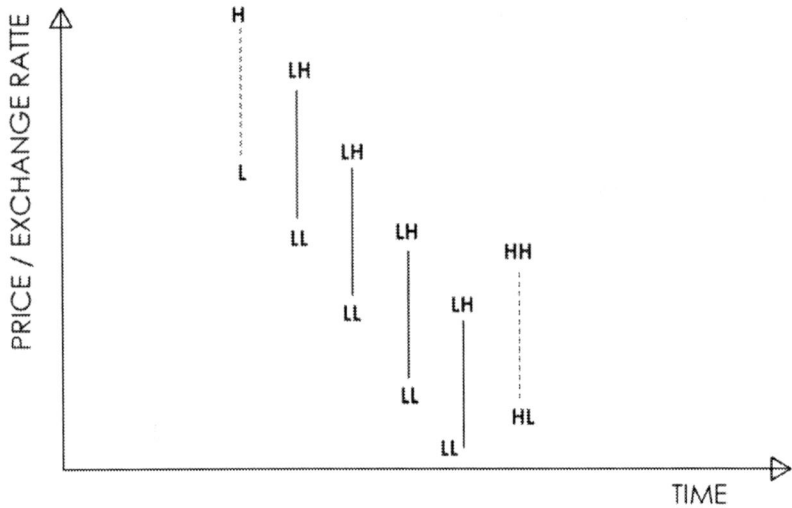

Image 12: Short-Term Bear Trends

Where: H – High, HH – Higher High, LH – Lower High, L – Low, LL –Lower Low, HL – Higher Low.

There is a bear trend as long as the price keeps making lower highs and lower lows. As soon as there is a higher high and a higher low, the short-term bull trend has finished.

Long-Term Trends: The Bull, Bear And The Crab Markets

There are three types of long-term trends: the bull, bear and the crab trend. The bull trend happens when the price makes a trending move upwards. The bear trend happens when the price makes a trending move downwards. The crab trend is when the market just moves sideways.

HOW TO IDENTIFY LONG-TERM BULL TRENDS:

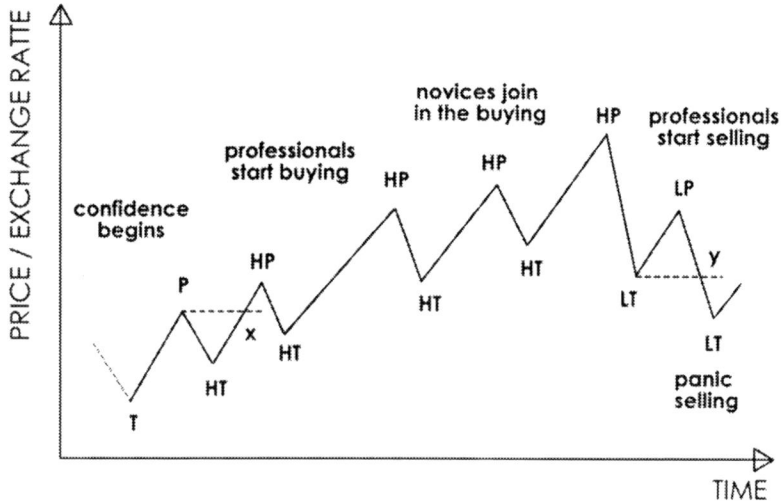

Image 13: Long-Term Bull Trends

Where: H – Higher, L – Lower, P – Peak and T-Trough.

- At point (x), the market breaks through the previous peak and makes a higher peak.
- It then makes a higher trough. This signals the beginning of a bull trend.
- Confidence begins to build up and the professionals start buying.
- After that, the novices notice the trend and they join in the buying.
- The professionals start selling their positions soon afterwards when they think the trend has weakened.
- The market makes a lower trough and then it goes up to a lower peak.
- This is followed by more selling as more people realise that the bull trend is ending.

- At point (y), the bull trend has finished because the price did go below the lower trough.

HOW TO IDENTIFY LONG-TERM BEAR TRENDS:

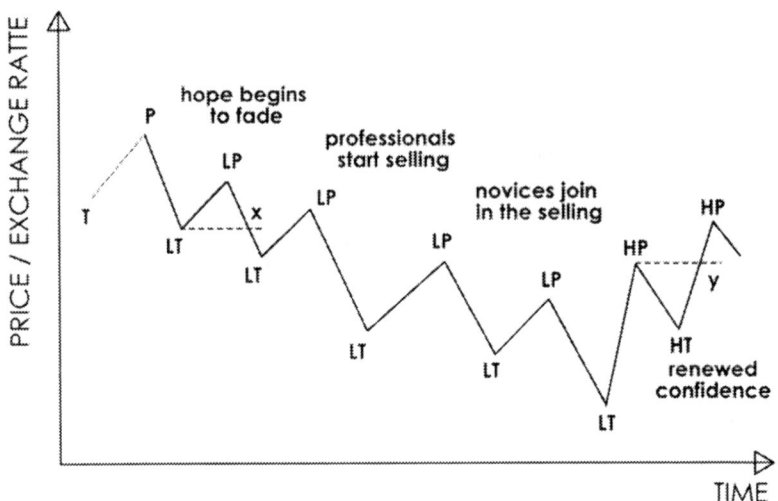

Image 14: Long-Term Bear Trend

Where: H – Higher, L – Lower, P – Peak and T-Trough.

- At the start of the chart, the market breaks through the previous trough to make a lower trough.
- It then makes a lower peak.
- The beginning of the bear trend is confirmed after the market goes under the lower trough at point (x).
- The professionals start selling.
- After that, the novices join in.
- Selling volume dissipates and eventually, the market becomes more saturated with buy orders. This applies an 'upward' pressure on the exchange rate. The price begins to rise.
- The market makes a higher peak.
- At point (y), the bear trend is finished because the market goes higher than the previous higher peak.

Of course, in real life, these trends are never that easy to identify because there are times when the market just stays in a crab trend and does not go anywhere. However, it is important to know because when you look at charts, you see these patterns emerge a lot. It also gives you a good description of what trends are. There are a few traders who use only these patterns as a basis for opening trades and exiting their positions.

HOW TO IDENTIFY LONG-TERM CRAB TRENDS:

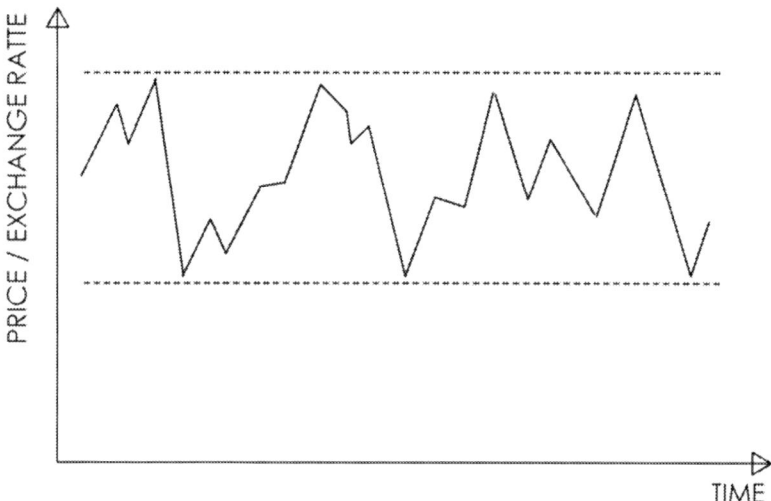

Image 15: Crab Market

A 'crab' market is when the market just traverses sideways, oscillating in a channel, between an imaginary 'floor' level and an imaginary 'ceiling' level.

CHAPTER 10: HOW TO ANALYSE CHARTS USING 'CLASSICAL CHARTING' TECHNIQUES

Sometimes people refer to technical analysts as 'chartists'. However, you should make a distinction between technical analysis and classical charting. Technical analysis uses indicators. These indicators are tedious to calculate without the aid of computers. Conversely, classical charting techniques are easily drawn by hand. They use the chart patterns and the line techniques we will discuss below.

TRENDLINES

Trendlines are lines connecting several extreme points on a chart. They are the simplest tools used to convey the general trend of the market. We need to consider a few things when we construct a trendline:
- We need a valid trend that is defined by the highs and lows or peaks and troughs created by the price movement,
- We need to anchor upward trendlines to the lows or troughs of the uptrend and we anchor downward trendlines to the highs or peaks of the downtrend and
- It becomes a valid trendline if the market recognises it the third time it approaches it. These recognition points could be 3 lows or troughs (if it is a bullish trendline) or 3 highs or peaks (if it is a bearish trendline).

- Without fulfilling these requirements, it is not a valid trendline…just a tentative one.

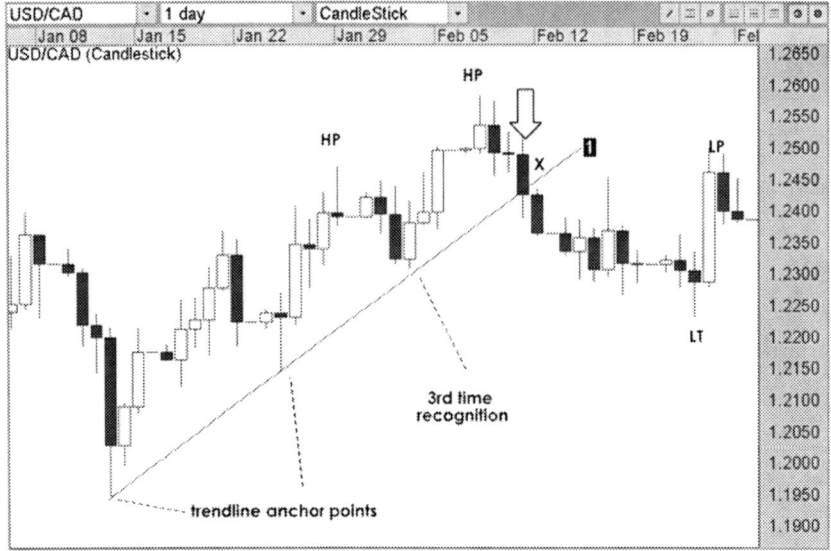

Image 16: Trendline

Consider how the upward trendline is constructed above:
- We see two troughs where we anchor the tentative trendline to.
- We see a higher peak and then we see that other market participants have recognised the trendline three times. This confirms that this is a valid trendline.
- The price breaks through the trendline downwards. This is marked (x) on the chart. This symbolises the end of the trend.

Sometimes trends accelerate or decelerate and trendlines can help you detect those movements. Below is an example of an accelerating trend.

Image 17: Accelerating Trendlines

When a trend line breaks, it is signalling the prevailing trend will soon be over. So what do you do when a trend line breaks? You may choose to close your position if the price closes below the trendline. I have marked three potential areas where some traders could have placed their stop-loss orders. Some traders use incremental exits to 'lighten' their positions also. These types of traders may have chosen to sell part of their entire position after the third trendline has been breached and sell some more after the price has gone under the second trendline. They can sell the rest after the price has punctured the first trendline.

SUPPORT AND RESISTANCE LEVELS

Support Levels

A support level is a price level where the downward movement of price reverses. This is a point where the buyers overpower the sellers in volume. They become more desperate than the sellers so they begin to buy at higher prices. This happened at points x, y and z on the chart below. The dashed line is the support level.

Image 18: Support Levels

To understand how a support level develops let us analyse what could have happened in the above chart.

- After the price rises from point (x) on the chart, some people begin realising that had they bought at point (x), they would have made a profit.
- The people who have traded downwards[37] at point (x) begin losing money afterwards and will want to close their trades as soon as the market goes back to point (x) where they can close their trades at break-even.
- Both types of people wait for the market to reach point (y) where they begin buying to open upward trades and to cover any 'short' positions they may have.
- This flurry of buying propels the price upwards as you can see after point (y) on the chart.
- After point (z), there are more people buying than there are selling, evident by the upward movement of the price. Among these 'bulls' are participants who may already have long trades but just wanted to add to their positions so they buy more.

---

[37] Trading downwards or going 'short' in this example means buy the CHF and sell the GBP.

Resistance Levels

A resistance level is a price level where the upward movement of price reverses. This is a point where the sellers overpower the buyers. They become more desperate than the buyers and so they begin to sell at lower prices. This happens twice in the example below, at points (x) and (y).

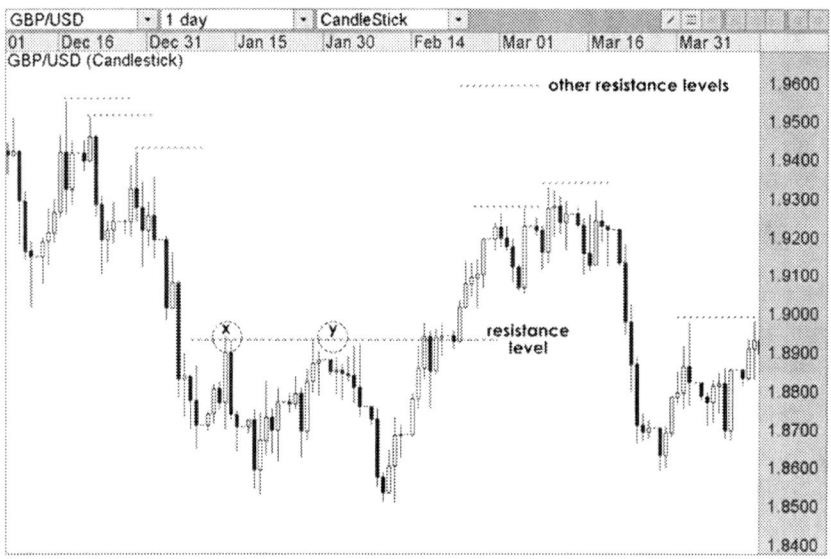

Image 19: Resistance Levels

To understand how a resistance level develops, let us consider the chart above.

- After point (x), the price sinks lower.
- Some people will start realising that had they traded downwards[38] at point (x), they would already be profiting.
- They wait until the market goes back to that level where they can open a downward trade.
- At the same time, people who thought the price was going to go up at point (x), start realising that they have opened trades facing the wrong direction. They will wait for the market to get

---

[38] Trading downwards or going 'short' in this example means to buy the USD and sell the GBP.

close to where they bought so they can sell at a price that is close enough to break even.
- Both parties wait for the market to reach point (y) where some begin opening 'short' trades and others begin to close their 'long' trades. All this selling will apply a downward pressure on the price, which eventually declines.

REVERSALS OF SUPPORT AND RESISTANCE (S-R) LEVELS

Once breached, a support level may become a resistance level and what may have been a resistance level may become a support level.

How Does Resistance Become Support?

In the example below, what used to be a resistance level becomes a support level.

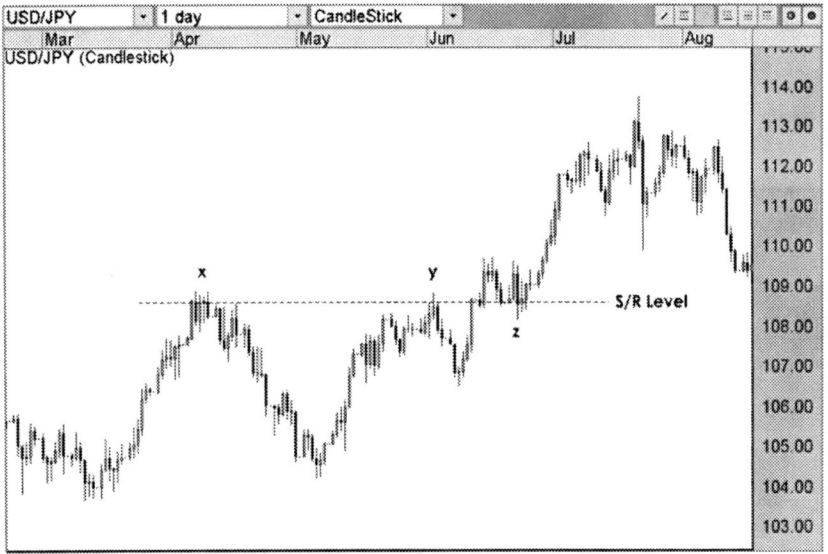

Image 20: Resistance Becomes Support

- Let's say you are one of the people who trade downwards at points (x) or at point (y).

- After the market breaks through the resistance level and closes above it, you and many other people would be in a losing position.
- The market stays above what used to be the resistance level and doubt begins to set in.
- Some 'bears' begin to close their 'short' positions to cut their losses.
- After a few days, more and more 'bears' start covering their 'short' positions. These events take place around the area marked (z).
- Eventually, traders and investors who had no positions will start buying after they are convinced the downward trend is over. They will become 'bulls' because of their optimistic belief in the USD.
- Market participants who used to be 'bearish' in their outlook will change their opinions about the direction of the market. Some will begin to join in the buying also.
- More and more people begin buying until it becomes clear there are more 'bulls' than 'bears' in the market.
- The 'bulls' prevail and as they get stronger, they propel the price upwards. What used to be a resistance level has just become a support level.

How Does Support Become Resistance?

Image 21: Support Becomes Resistance

Here is a good example of how long people remember old support and resistance levels. This formation develops over the course of 10 months.

- At point (w) and (x), many people have decided to buy around the 1.8500 level, where there has been support.
- We can tell there have been a significant number of people who bought around the 1.8500 level because of the number of times the market lingered at that price level. People bought at that price during November, January, February and late March.
- The best time for traders to take profits would have been in March or late April.
- The traders who did not take profits would have been nervous after the price fell through the support level in May.
- Traders who had a 'long' position with an entry price greater than 1.8500 would have started to incur losses. As the market hits its most extreme level around 1.7300 during mid-July, many of these trades would have been suffering massive losses.

- Many would have made a vow that as soon as the market gives them the opportunity to close their 'long' trades at a small loss, they would do so.
- For many traders, the pain would have been so severe that they would have closed their 'long' trades at tremendous losses.
- By September, the market did go back close enough to the 1.18500 level. Here, people flooded the market with sell orders to close 'long' trades and to open downward trades.
- People who wished they traded downward after point (y) will join in the selling, at point (z), too.
- The 'bears' grow stronger and the price dives down. What used to be a support level has just become a resistance level.

TREND CHANNELS

A trend channel is a trendline with a parallel line above (if it is a 'bullish' trendline) or below it (if it is a 'bearish' trendline). For there to be a valid channel, there must be a valid trendline. The minimum requirements for a channel are shown below:

For a 'bullish' channel	For a 'bearish' channel
Two troughs	Two peaks
An intervening high	An intervening trough
A rise above the intervening peak to validate the second trough	A fall below the intervening trough to validate the second peak

To illustrate how a channel is created, below is an example of a 'bear' channel.

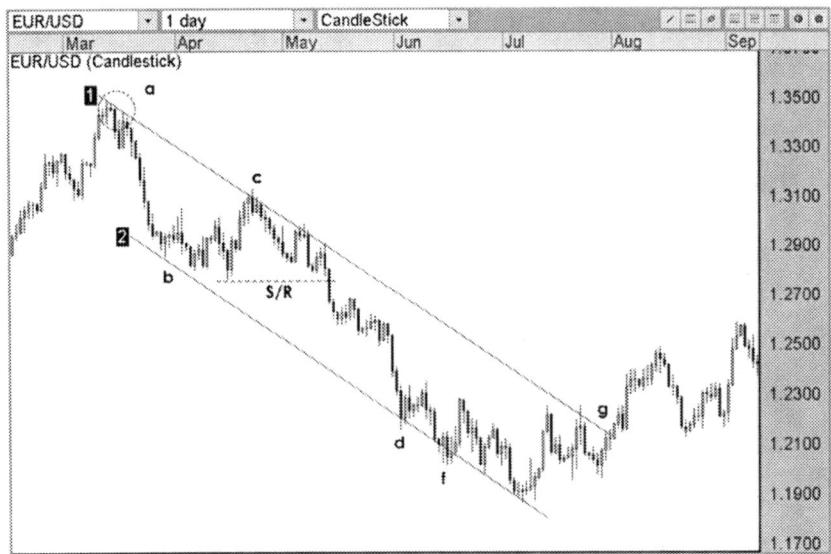

Image 22: Trend Channels

- A valid trendline needs to be confirmed by three highs or three peaks.
- In the circle at point (a), the price confirms this criterion because of the three highs that confirm the trendline. The bearish trendline is valid.
- At point (b), the prices make an intervening trough, which later becomes a support-resistance level.
- The market goes up to point (c) where it confirms the bearish trendline again.
- It then drops below the most recent support level.
- As soon as it hits point (d), and begins going up, we have a trend channel.

CHART PATTERNS

Classical chartists see chart patterns as heads and shoulders, double tops and bottoms, triple tops and bottoms, rectangles, triangles, wedges and flags. I am not going to discuss those here because they are merely applications of the logic behind trendlines, channels and support-resistance levels.

Just in case you wanted to know, I only look at trendlines, trend channels and support-resistance levels. I do not try to identify chart patterns because I find that they need much subjectivity. An analyst may see patterns because of what he wants to see, even if the patterns are not there. The human mind has a tendency to conjure up patterns from random data. The best example of this was when people began connecting stars into constellations.

One way around this lack of objectivity is to tell a computer to scan the markets for such patterns. By doing this, you can get statistics about how successful these patterns may have been in the past. The difficulty with this is that it's hard to define what patterns are. You know one when you see one, but to code it into computer language is no easy task for the average trader.

THE FLEXIBILITY OF CLASSICAL CHARTING LINE TECHNIQUES

Please note that the market may push the boundaries of trendlines, channels and support-resistance levels. If the market crosses any of these lines, it does not instantly mean that they have been breached. They are not like glass barriers in the charts that 'shatter' just because the price pierces through them. You can best think of trendlines, channels and support-resistance levels as fences. The price may pierce through them, poke through them a little, push their boundaries and still manage to bounce back.

ENTERING TRADES USING CLASSICAL CHARTING

You may open a trade based on classical charting analysis techniques using trendlines, channels and support-resistance levels. The diagram below is an example of how you can open trades based on such analysis.

Image 23: Entering Trades Using Classical Charting Analysis

In this example, you can see that you can trade trend channels, which are essentially parallel support-resistance levels.

- After the market bounces away from a support level, a trader may open an upward trade, like the event in point (b) on the chart.
- At point (c), buyers have tried to push through the previous resistance level made after point (a).
- After realising the buyers' resolve has begun to dissipate, the sellers drive the market down.
- The arrows drawn within the channel are potential profitable trades made by traders who engage in what is sometimes referred to as counter-trend trading. The idea behind this trading strategy is to buy at the low of the channel and sell at the high of the channel.
- A trader who tries to profit after price breaks out from flat markets practices trend-trading.
- The types of trades they profit from occur in break-outs like those in point (d) and (e) on the chart.
- Notice the breakout that occurred at point (d) was a false breakout.
- At point (e) there has been a real breakout.

EXITING TRADES USING CLASSICAL CHARTING

This method sets stop-losses using classical charting line techniques like trendlines, channels and support-resistance levels.

Image 24: Exiting Using Classical Charting Methods – Profit

Consider the example above:

- We simply assume to have entered the trade at the bottom left, marked by the upward arrow;
- If we are using trendlines as our exit trigger, then we would have closed the trade at a profit, at point (B) on the chart;
- If we are using support-resistance levels then we would have been able to get out at a profit when the price pierces down a support-resistance level, like it did in point (C) on the chart;
- Let us say we have missed the exit points at point (B) or (C), we can still get out after the breakout occurs at the end of the trading channel at point (D) on the chart.

Image 25: Using The 'Classical' Method - Loss

Consider the example above:

- The trader enters at point (A) because he thinks the market will go up since a resistance level has just been broken.
- He places a trade and puts a stop-loss level at the previous support level so that when the trade does not go his way, he would get out.
- The trader gets taken out of the trade at point (B) on the chart.

CHAPTER 11: YOUR TOOLS, TECHNICAL INDICATORS

Technical indicators are mathematical calculations derived from the prices (open, close, high and low) of any tradeable instrument. In our case, our instruments are currencies. These calculations are plotted on a chart using computers so that we, as technical analysts, can interpret these calculations visually. By using indicators, we are simplifying many thousands of mathematical calculations and concepts in visual terms that our brain is able to process easily.

There are a plethora of indicators to choose from. Indicators are the tools of an analyst regardless of whether he is using fundamental analysis or technical analysis. I will take you through how to use them.

The Objectivity Of Indicators

Indicators are calculated mathematically. Therefore, unlike classical charting techniques, they do not involve much subjectivity. An analyst is likely to get a more objective signal than when he is only using classical charting techniques.

Indicators Do Not Predict, They Measure

Based on the way some people use indicators, it is almost as if they are working on the belief that technical indicators are able to predict the future. Technical indicators should merely be used as measuring tools to measure the changes in price. It is important for you to be able to identify which notion you are acting under. Are you using indicators as tools to try to predict the future or as tools to measure price movement? As a trader, your approach to developing your own methodology will change dramatically once you identify this elementary difference.

Simplicity Of Indicators

It does not necessarily mean that a particular indicator is better for you just because it is more complex. I have tried and tested many indicators. In the beginning, I had been drawn to the more complex indicators. However, over the years, I have become more reliant on the basic ones. There are a couple of reasons for this. Firstly, I can count on them to be included in any charting software and trading platform I may use. Secondly, they are easier to code into computer language when it is time to test my ideas. So, when it comes to indicators, simple ones are not necessarily inferior. Instead, they are easy, straightforward, uncomplicated and undemanding to work with. Trading is not all about using indicators. Indicators are only a small part of the process, so this book takes you through the simple ones that I use.

THE INDICATOR FAMILIES

There are primarily two families of indicators. They are:

1. Trend-following indicators
    a. The Moving Average (MA)
        i. Single MA
        ii. Dual MA

2. Momentum oscillators
    i. Stochastic Oscillator;
    ii. The Williams % R,
    iii. The Commodity Channel Index

We will also discuss the MACD indicator which is a trend-following indicator as well as an oscillator.

TREND-FOLLOWING INDICATORS

The main strengths of these indicators are to identify trends and profit from them. They are most effective when the market is trending either up or down. In crab markets, they perform horribly.

THE MOVING AVERAGE (MA)

The moving average smoothens out the price action. It is constructed by calculating the averages of the price over the last x number of bars from any given bar. The shorter the number of days, the more sensitive the moving average is to the movements of the price. We calculate the average every day and plot these values on the chart. If we are to connect these average points, we get what looks like a curvy line.

The averages are usually calculated using the close price of every bar or candlestick. You might also come across different types of moving averages like simple, time-series, triangular, variable, volume-adjusted, weighted and exponential moving averages. To keep our examples straightforward, we will only use simple moving averages. It is easier to calculate when you test your ideas.

SIGNALS:
- Buy when price is above the moving average.
- Sell when price is below the moving average.

Below is an example of how a moving average is plotted on the daily chart of the GBP/USD and how a trader can use this to trade the currency pair. I used a 144-bar moving average. That means the moving average that you see represents the moving average of the most recent 144 bars.

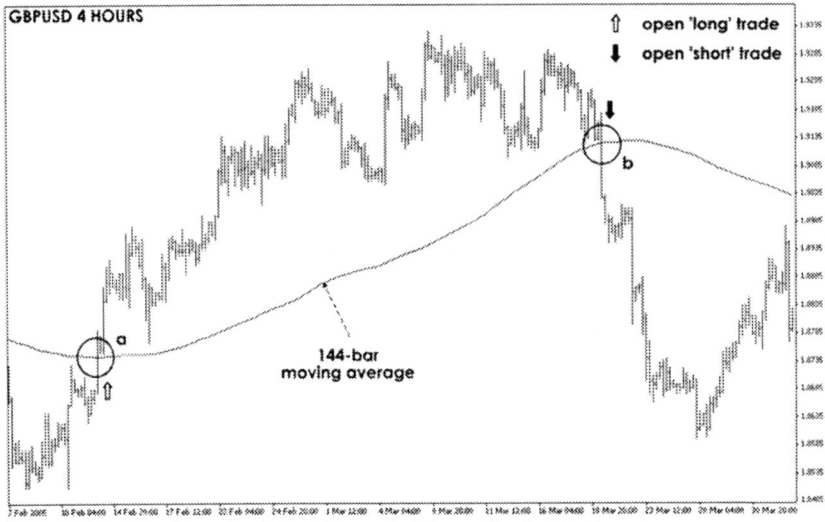

Image 26: The Buy And Sell Signals Given By A Moving Average

Consider the chart above:

- A trader can open a 'long' trade when the price crosses above the moving average at point (a).
- After that, the trader can close his upward trade at a profit where the price crosses the moving average at point (b) on the chart.
- At the same time, the trader may also want to open a downward trade at this point to profit when the market goes down.

'Whipsaws'

A 'whipsaw' is a false signal that happens when an indicator sends out a signal to enter the market and another signal to get out of the market, before the trade has had any chance of becoming profitable. Whipsaws therefore, often result in losses. They happen when prices move up and down so quickly that the indicator cannot keep up. All indicators give out false signals but they are a lot more problematic with trend-following indicators.

Image 27: A 'Whipsaw' On A Moving Average

Consider the chart above:

- The price triggers a signal for us to open a downward trade when the price crosses under the moving average at point (a) on the chart.
- We open a 'short' trade hoping for a profit but the market never goes down long enough and far enough.
- It makes a u-turn, triggering us to close our 'short' trade when the price crosses over the moving average at point (b) on the chart.

This problem becomes severe when we use a moving average that has a shorter time-frame. In the example below, I will run a 21-bar moving average on the daily chart of the USD/JPY.

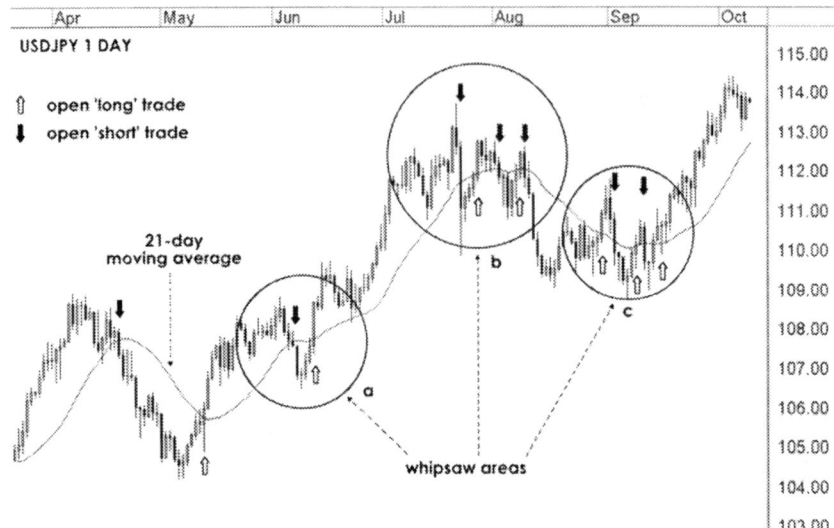

Image 28: Whipsaws & Shorter Moving Averages

Note how many whipsaws occurred in the three different whipsaw areas on the chart above. Each of those signals could have costed the trader a lot.

Using Filters To Minimise Whipsaws

We can use a filter to reduce the number of times we go in and out of whipsaw areas. To do this we have to add another rule to say that we are not going to buy or sell just because the price has gone above or below the moving average. By adding another rule, we filter out market 'noise'.

Here are examples of filtering rules you can use:

1. The price must close across the moving average;
2. The price must close across the moving average two days or three days in a row;
3. The slope of the moving average: an upward slope confirms that it is fine to go 'long'; a downward slope confirms that it is fine to go 'short' and a flat slope suggests you should probably stay out and wait for a better signal;

4. The price must cross the moving average by a certain percentage of the price or the moving average; and
5. One entire bar must have crossed above or below the moving average.

The best way to find out which filter would be good is to test each one separately on the charts you wish to trade.

The 'Lag Effect' Of Technical Indicators

Trend-following indicators are trailing indicators. They lag the movement of the price and because of this, the signals they give come too late to capitalise on making profits from short-term trends. By having delayed signals, a trader's profitability gets damaged.

The Sensitivity Of The MA, The 'Lag Effect' And 'Whipsaws'

Using a shorter moving average has the following effect:
- We increase the sensitivity of the moving average to the movements of the price.
- Therefore, we decrease the lag effect and as a result, we get the signals earlier.
- We increase the number of times we get 'whipsawed' in and out of the market.

Using a longer moving average has the following effect:
- We decrease the sensitivity of the moving average to the movements of the price.
- Therefore, we get the signals later. We increase the lag effect.
- We decrease the number of times we get 'whipsawed' in and out of the market.

To prove this, I will add a shorter (5-day) moving average as well as a longer (55-day) moving average to the one 21-day moving average we used in the previous example.

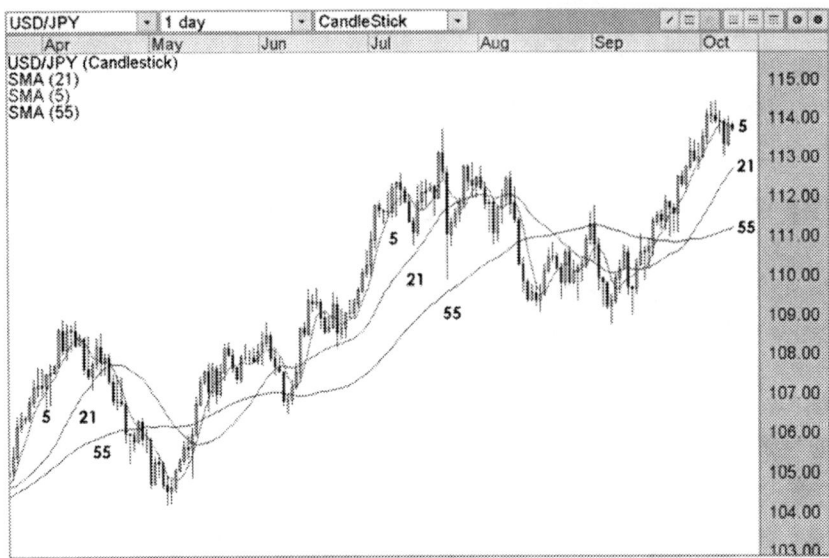

Image 29: Sensitivity, Lag Effect & Whipsaws

As you can see, if we use the shorter (5-day) moving average, we may catch the beginning and end of the trends earlier but we also get 'whipsawed' a lot. If we use the longer (55-day) moving average, we see that we catch the beginning and the ends of the trade a lot later but we get 'whipsawed' less.

DUAL MOVING AVERAGE

The single moving average has a weakness. It gives too many false signals. As we have discussed, one way around that is to use filters to filter out the market 'noise'. Another alternative is to use two moving-averages, each with different timeframes.

SIGNALS:
- Buy when the shorter moving average crosses under the longer moving average.

- Sell when the shorter moving average crosses above the longer moving average.

In the example below we use a 12-bar moving average as the shorter term moving-average and a 26-bar moving average as the longer term moving-average.

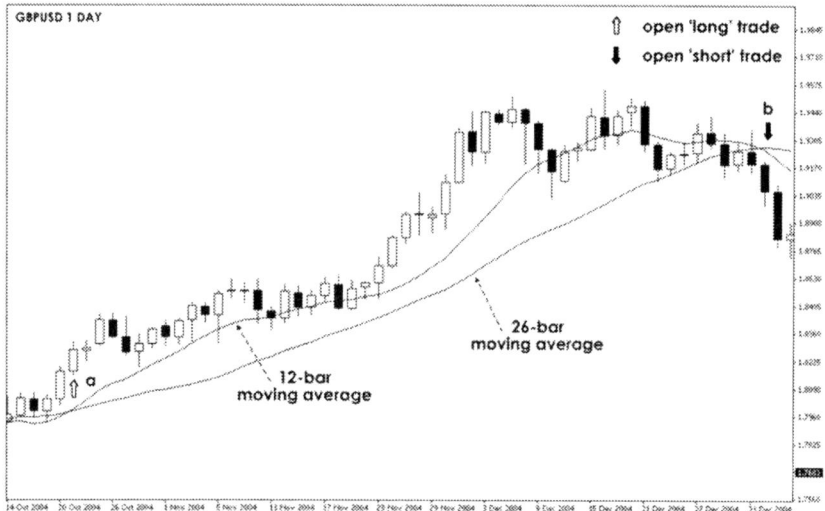

Image 30: Dual Moving Average Performing In An Ideal Scenario

- We only open a 'long' trade the day after the shorter moving average crosses above the longer moving average, marked (a) on the chart and
- We close the trade when the shorter moving average crosses under the longer moving average, marked (b) on the chart.

The example below shows you how the two moving averages behave when the market is a little bit more volatile.

Image 31: Dual Moving Average Performing In A More Volatile Market

If we did not use a dual-moving average strategy, we would have suffered several whipsaws, which would have resulted in many losing trades.

SENTIMENT-BASED OSCILLATORS

The rate at which price changes, is called: momentum. When the price accelerates in one direction, then its momentum increases. If the price slows down, then its momentum decreases.

The main purpose of oscillators is to give the trader a visual summary of price momentum. The goal is to try to give you accurate signals to buy at the low of a trading channel and sell at the high of a trading channel.

Sentiment-based oscillators are also known as momentum oscillators, or counter-trend indicators. They swing back and forth, or up and down, across a reference point that is usually zero or between two boundaries.

Zero Oscillators may look like this:

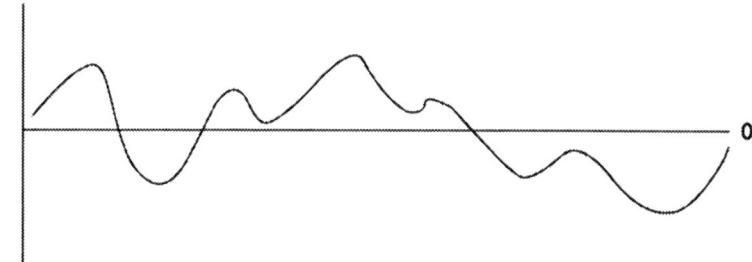

Image 32: Zero Oscillators

Boundary oscillators may look like this:

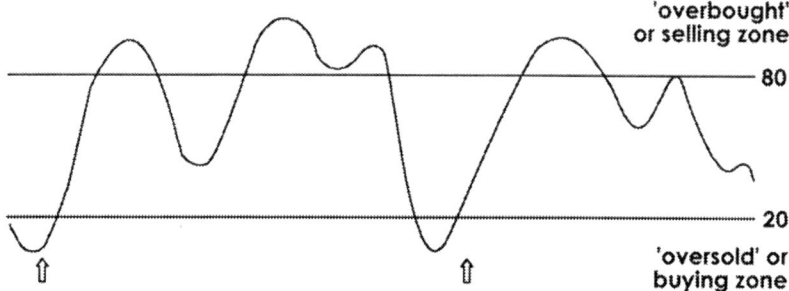

Image 33: Boundary Oscillators

PLEASE NOTE:
In this example, the buying and selling zones are 20 and 80 respectively. I prefer to refer to them as the **'lower'** and the **'upper'** level. Other indicators have different levels. We call these **overbought** and **oversold** zones. However, I find it less confusing when I refer to them as **buying zones** and **selling zones**.

Bullish Oscillator Signals:

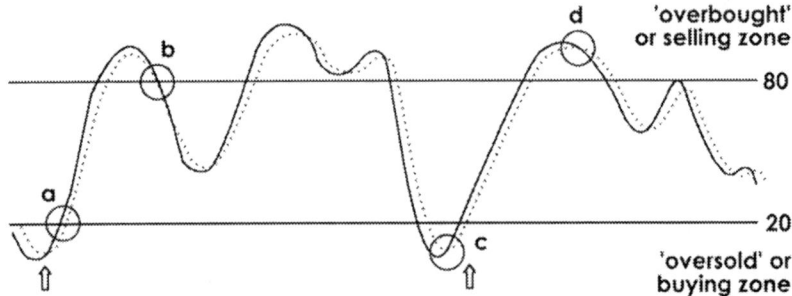

Image 34: Bullish Oscillator Signals

Signals:

1. Swing Trades

Buy when the indicator goes above the lower level at point (a). If it makes a U-turn before going to the selling zone, you may exit. If it successfully gets to the selling zone, you wait until it crosses under the selling zone level of 80 (point b) to exit.

2. Crossover Signal

This signal would only be possible if you are dealing with an oscillator that has two lines. You buy when the two lines cross over (point c). You sell when they cross again (point d). If you use this method, you may also choose to buy and sell during crossovers without worrying about whether the indicator is in the buying or selling zone.

3. Zero Signal

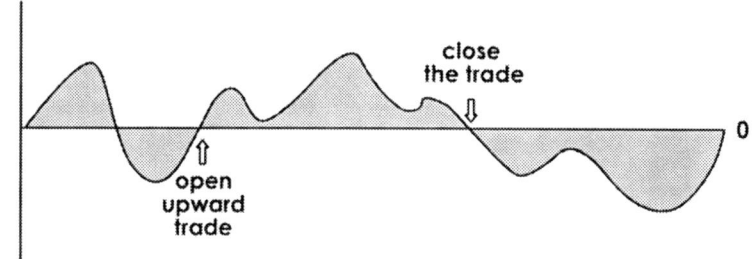

Image 35: Zero Bullish Oscillator Signals

Signals:

The signals of these types of indicators signal where you can go 'long' and open an upward trade when it is positive.

4. Bullish Divergence Signals

Divergence is a signal given by oscillators that other traders use to spot potential opportunities to trade. Divergence signals occur when the price and an oscillator do not confirm each other.

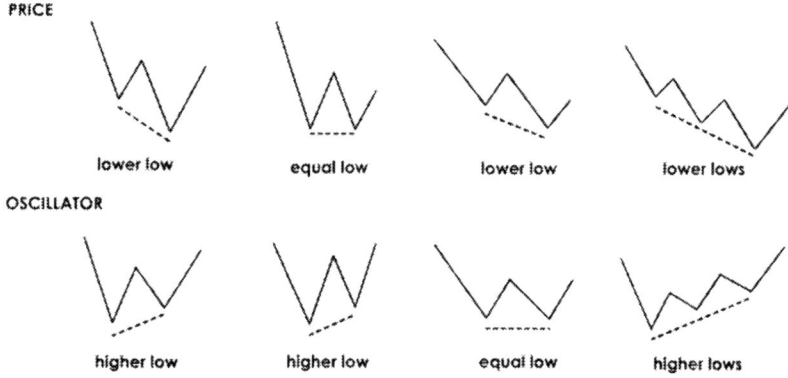

Image 36: Bullish Divergences Between Price And An Oscillator

Bearish Oscillator Signals

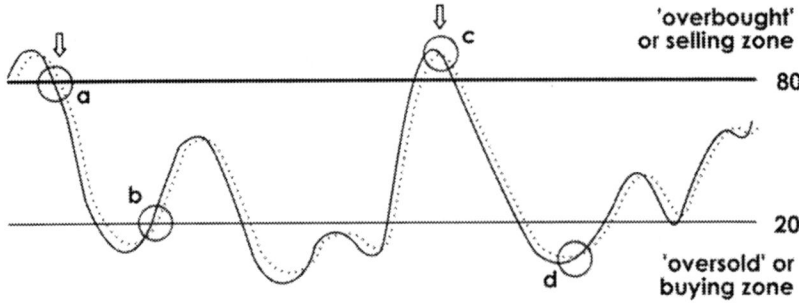

Image 37: Bearish Oscillator Signals

Signals:

1. **Swing Trades**

You may 'short' sell when the indicator goes under the upper level (point a). If it makes a u-turn before going to the buying zone, you may exit. If it successfully gets to the buying zone, you wait until it crosses over the buying zone level of 20 (point b) to exit.

2. **Crossover**

You may 'short' sell when the two lines cross over (point c). You close when they cross over again (point d). If you use this method, you may choose to buy and sell during crossovers without worrying about whether the indicator is in the buying or selling zone.

3. Zero Signal

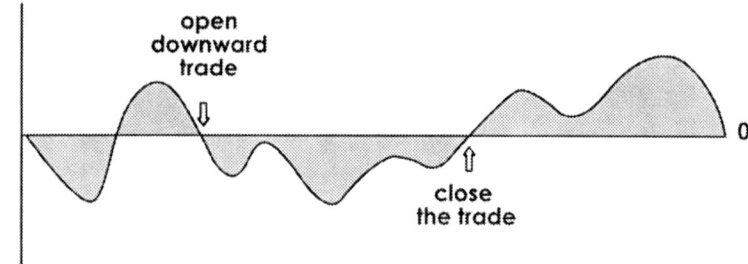

Image 38: Bearish Zero Oscillator Signals

Signals:

The signals of these types of indicators could signal where you can go 'short' and open a downward trade when the indicator is negative.

4. Bearish Divergence Signals

Divergence is a signal given by oscillators that other traders use to spot potential opportunities to trade. Divergence signals occur when the price and an oscillator do not confirm each other.

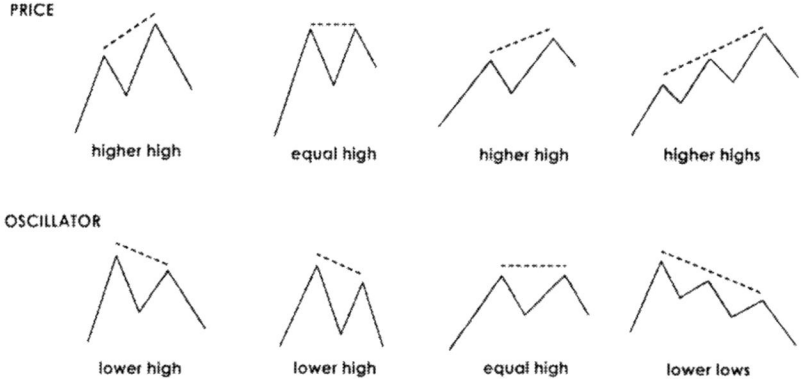

Image 39: Bearish Divergence Signals Between Price And An Oscillator

THE STOCHASTIC OSCILLATOR

The Stochastic Oscillator is an indicator developed by George C. Lane in the late 1950s. The theory behind this indicator is that in an upward-trending market, prices tend to close near their high, and during a downward-trending market, prices tend to close near their low.

This oscillator compares where price closes relative to its trading range over a given period. You can reduce the oscillator's sensitivity to market movements by adjusting the time period or by taking a moving average of the result. Its formula:

$$\%K = (C - Low(n)) / (High(n) - Low(n))$$

C = the most recent closing price
Low(n) = the lowest low over the past n periods
High(n) = the highest high over the past n periods
n = the number of periods, typically 14.

Transaction signals occur when a variable called '%K' crosses through a three-period moving average called the '%D'. Below is a real-life example of a Stochastic Oscillator that is applied to a 15-minute chart of the GBP/USD.

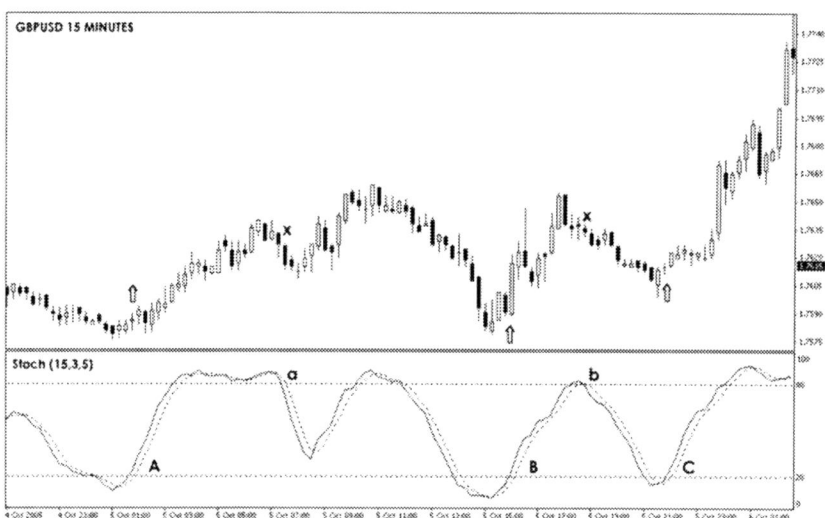

Image 40: The Stochastic Oscillator

Consider the following example:

- Let us assume that you are only going to take the '**swing trade**' entry and exit signals.
- You only take 'long' trades, meaning you only take upward trades and you ignore downward signals.
- The oscillator is telling you to get in at point (A) on the price chart, this is marked by the arrow.
- At point (a), you close the trade.
- The second trade is opened at point (B).
- You close it at point (b) on the oscillator.
- At point (C), you would have opened an upside trade just in time to catch the upside break-out at the end of the chart.

THE WILLIAMS' % R

This indicator was developed by Larry Williams. The formula used to calculate the value of the Williams %R is:

%R = (High(*n*) – Close) / (High(*n*) – Low(*n*))

Where: High(*n*) = The highest high over *n* periods
Low(*n*) = The lowest low over *n* periods
n = the number of periods we want to calculate

The unusual property of this indicator is that it is plotted on an upside-down scale with 0 at the top and 100 at the bottom. Why I look at this indicator is because it has an uncanny ability to anticipate a reversal in the underlying security's price. To witness this, look at the graph below:

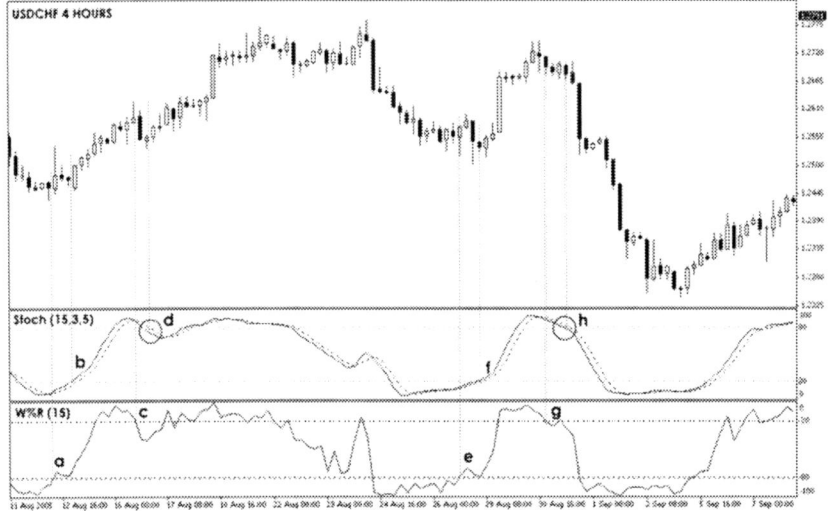
Image 41: Using The Stochastic Oscillator And The Williams'%R Together

In this example, we are using the same length of 15 bars for both indicators and yet, as you can see, the Williams'%R is always a pace ahead of the Stochastic Oscillator. On this 4-hour chart, it makes a signal about 12 hours ahead of the Stochastic every time.

So why don't we just use the Williams'%R and get rid of the Stochastic? Looking at the graph, the Williams'%R is too volatile. It keeps oscillating up and down. It can get difficult knowing which signals you should take as a trigger to take action. The Stochastic Oscillator on the other hand, helps us get a 'smoothened' feel for the momentum of the price. Together, they can keep a check on each other. What one indicator tells you, the other should confirm. One way to use them both is to allow Williams'%R to alert you of what might be ahead. As soon as the Stochastic confirms the same verdict, you can carry out the appropriate action with confidence.

THE COMMODITY CHANNEL INDEX (CCI)

Developed by Donald Lambert, the Commodity Channel Index (CCI) was designed to identify cyclical turns of the market. To calculate, we go through the following steps:

1) Calculate the last period's Typical Price (TP) = (H+L+C)/3 where H = high, L = low, and C = close;
2) Calculate the *n*-period Simple Moving Average of the Typical Price (SMATP). (*n* is the number of periods that you choose. The value of this will depend on the chart you are studying. You can only find out by testing.)
3) Calculate the Mean Deviation. First, calculate the absolute value of the difference between the last period's SMATP and the typical price for each of the past *n* periods. Add all of these absolute values together and divide by *n* to find the Mean Deviation.
4) The final step is to apply the Typical Price (TP), the Simple Moving Average of the Typical Price (SMATP), the Mean Deviation and a Constant (.015) to the following formula:

CCI = [(Typical Price) − (SMATP)] / [(.0015) x (Mean Deviation)]

Again, you do not have to calculate all these yourself because most charting programs and most brokers provide this indicator in their trading platforms already. The example below shows you what it looks like and how we use it much like we use any other indicator.

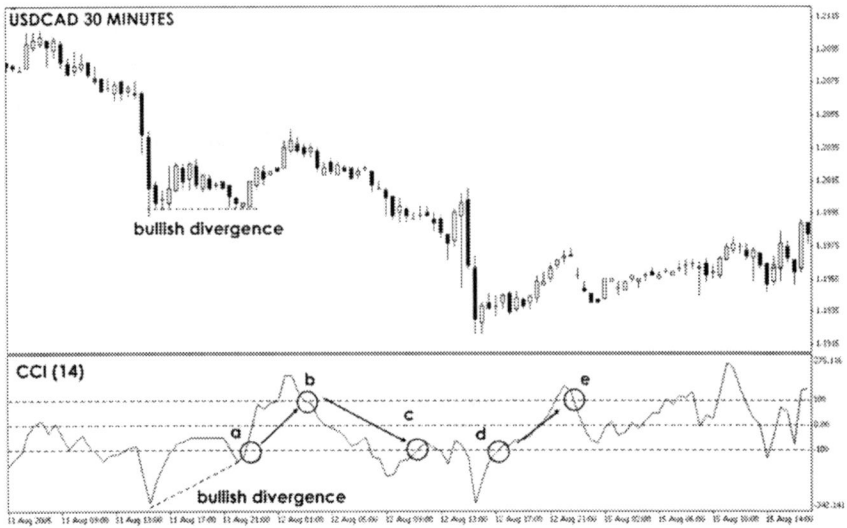
Image 42: The CCI

Look at the CCI in the example above:

- There was a bullish divergence at the beginning of the chart.
- There is a buy signal, marked (*a*) on the indicator. You close that trade at point (*b*).
- You may also decide to 'short' sell at point (*b*) and then close that trade at point (*c*).
- There was another buy signal, marked (*d*), and the closing signal, marked (*e*) on the chart.

Much like the Williams'%R, the CCI warns us of impending danger before the Stochastic does.

Oscillator Sensitivity, Whipsaws And The 'Lag Effect'

Each oscillator has its own given parameters. Charting packages and trading platforms usually provide you with the default values the creators of the indicators have recommended. The shorter timeframe you use for your parameters, the more sensitive your indicator becomes to the movements of price. This reduces the lag effect but signals more 'whipsaws'. By increasing the timeframe you use for your oscillator parameters, you reduce the sensitivity of your indicator to the movements of the price. This increases the 'lag effect' but it will signal fewer 'whipsaws'.

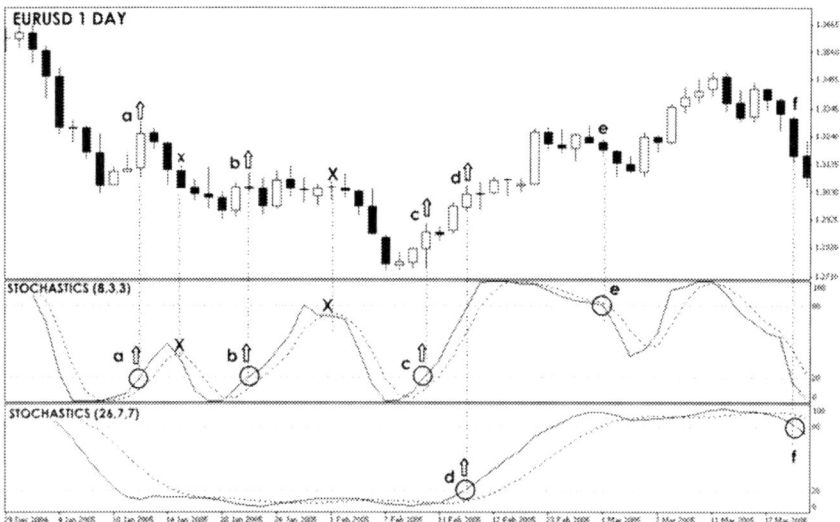

Image 43: Oscillator Sensitivity, Whipsaws & Lag Effect.

Look at the chart above:
- We use two Stochastic Oscillators: one with a shorter time frame and one with a longer timeframe.
- As you can see on the chart, the shorter Stochastic has triggered 3 buy signals but only one of them has been profitable. This trade is the one labelled (c) on the chart.
- The longer Stochastic has only one signal, trade (d).
- Notice the shorter Stochastic triggers more 'whipsaws'.
- The longer Stochastic has no 'whipsaws' but there is a longer delay in the signals than when we use a shorter oscillator.

THE MACD - MOVING AVERAGE CONVERGENCE DIVERGENCE

This is an indicator developed by Gerald Appel and is considered by many to be one of the simplest and most reliable indicators available. The MACD is both a trend following indicator and an oscillator.

Its origin comes from dual moving averages. As I have explained above, trading with two moving-averages improves the timing of the signals; however, the signals are still not given soon enough. Trends lose momentum by a great deal before the dual moving-average system tells the trader that it is time to take his profits. By then, most of the open profits would have been reduced to zero. Even worse, the market may have retracted so far back that the position could be incurring a loss by the time the signal to close the trade is given. The MACD helps alleviate most of this problem.

To calculate the MACD, we do the following steps:

1. MACD Line = shorter moving average − longer moving average.
2. We apply another moving average on the MACD Line. We call this the MACD Moving Average.
3. MACD = MACD Line − MACD Moving Average.
4. The MACD is plotted as a histogram for better visualisation.
5. A moving average can then be applied to measure the rate of change of the MACD Histogram. To distinguish this from the MACD Moving Average, we will call this the MACD Histogram Moving Average.

Where:
- The shorter moving average is usually a 12-bar moving average,
- The longer moving average is usually a 26-bar moving average.
- The MACD moving average is usually 9.

The characteristic of the MACD allows it to be used as a trend-following indicator as well as an oscillator.

Different Representations Of The MACD

Different charting packages and trading platforms display the MACD in various ways. Some will only show you the calculation results for step 3, others only show you the calculations for step 4. Step 3 and 4 MACDs are like the one shown below:

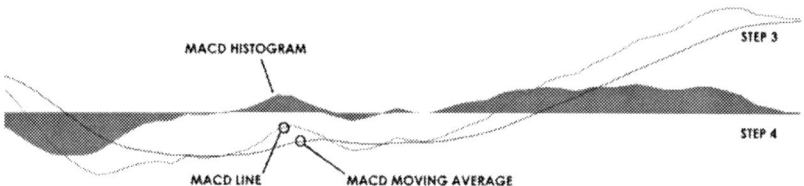

Image 44: MACD Using Step 3 & 4

We can see the following events in the chart above:

- When the MACD line is greater than the MACD Moving Average, the MACD Histogram is positive,
- If the MACD Moving Average is above the MACD Line, the MACD Histogram is negative.

Step 5 is just the MACD Histogram with a moving average applied to it like the diagram shown below.

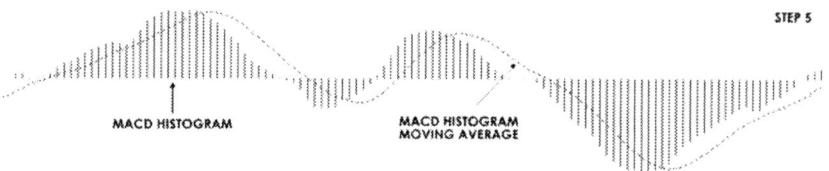

Image 45: MACD Using Step 5

This book assumes this method of representing MACD.

(*Please note the MACD Histograms from both illustrations are not based on the same data.*[39])

---

[39] At the time of writing, I am not aware of any program yet that is able to display the MACD in all three ways. Furthermore, different forex brokers do not have the exact same data. Such is the nature of the forex market, because it is not a centralized exchange. Not all brokers and data sources have the same price data.

SIGNALS OF THE MACD HISTOGRAM AND ITS MOVING AVERAGE

Signals:

Zero-Trigger

Buy when the indicator goes above zero. Sell when the indicator goes under zero.

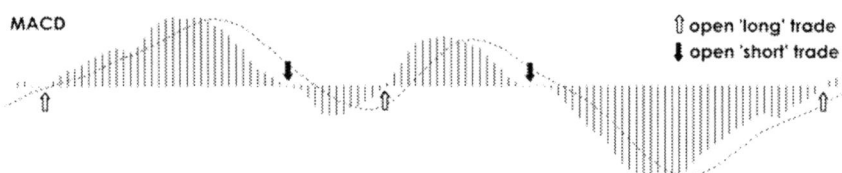

Image 46: MACD Zero Trigger

Crossover Signal

- Buy when the MACD Histogram crosses above the MACD Histogram Moving Average.
- Sell when the MACD Histogram crosses under the MACD Histogram Moving Average.

If you only have access to a MACD Histogram but you cannot run a moving average on it, then you will not be able to use this signal.

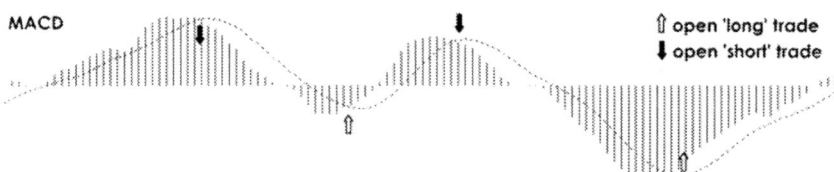

Image 47: MACD Cross-Over Signal

The Difference Between Zero-Trigger And Crossover MACD Signals

The reason I want to apply a moving average on the MACD Histogram is best illustrated below.

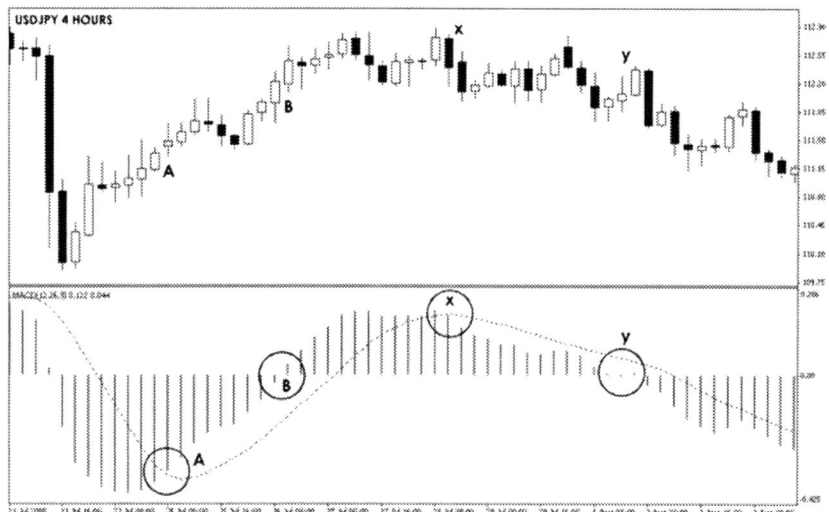
Image 48: Zero Trigger Vs. Crossover Signals

- For a charting program that can calculate the MACD Histogram Moving Average, you get a buy signal at point (A) on the chart and a selling signal at point (x).
- If your charting program cannot calculate a MACD Histogram Moving Average, you can only take the zero triggers. The open signal is marked (B) on the chart and the exit signal is marked (y). The crossover signals have been more profitable than the zero trigger signals.

Divergence Signals

Divergence is a signal given by oscillators that other traders use to spot potential opportunities to trade. Divergence signals occur when the price and an oscillator – like the MACD – do not confirm each other.

Below is a chart that gives you the bullish divergences between the price and the MACD:

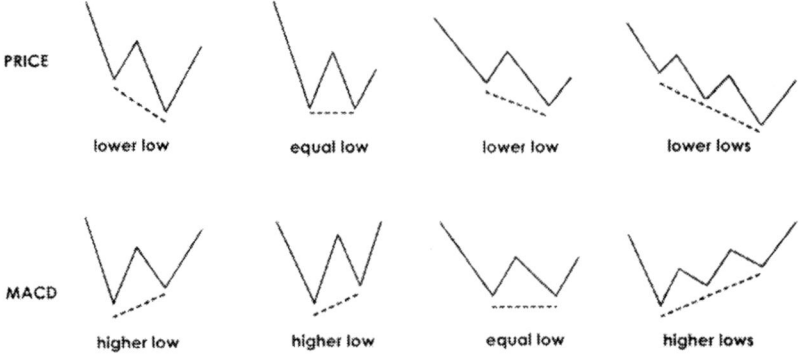

Image 49: MACD Bullish Divergences

Below is a chart that gives you the bearish divergences between the price and the MACD:

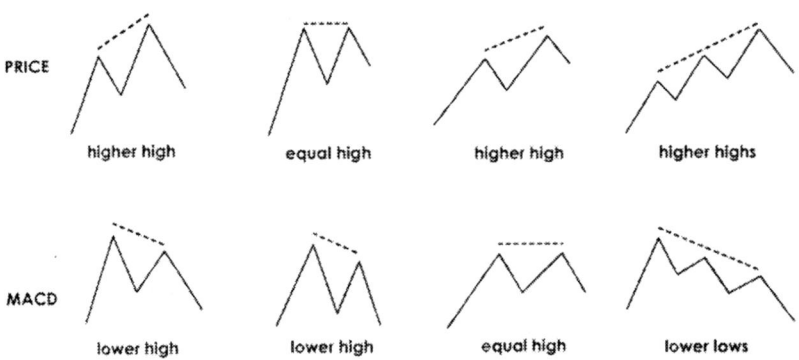

Image 50: MACD Bearish Divergences

The example below shows the examples of bullish divergences:

Image 51: Example Of A Bullish MACD Divergence Signals

- At the start of the graph, the slope of Line 1 and the slope of line A is what you would normally expect.
- As the price makes higher peaks, the MACD Histogram should be making new highs too.
- With Line 2 and Line B, there is a divergence. The price is making new troughs but the MACD Histogram is not. This is a 'bullish' signal and you should open a 'long' trade.
- The 'bullishness' of the signal is confirmed once again by another bullish divergence made with Line 3 and Line C. The price is making an equal trough but the MACD Histogram is making a higher trough.

Strengths & Weaknesses Of Indicators

Trend-following systems are great when there is a trend, but they constantly give off false signals as soon as the price starts oscillating sideways. Oscillators shine during flat, sideways markets but they give off bad signals and miss many profits as soon as the market erupts into a trend. This observation is highlighted with the example below.

Trading With Indicators

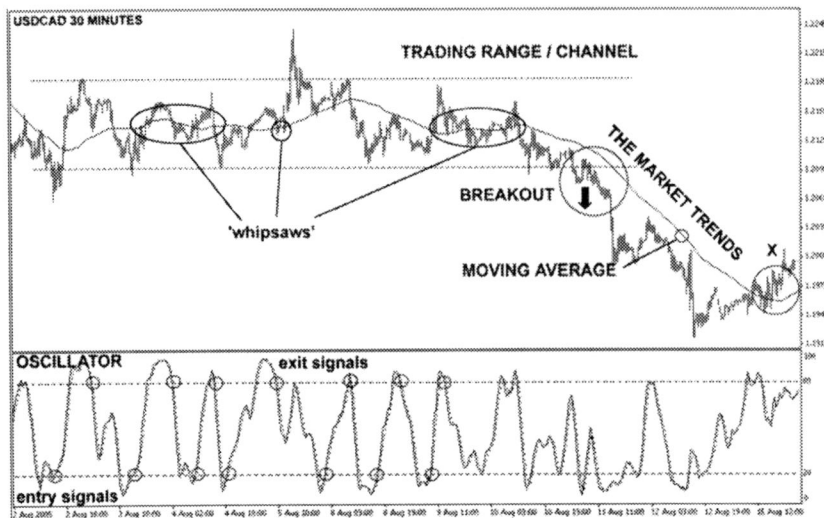

Image 52: Using Indicators Or Channels To Enter And Exit The Market

The chart above shows you how a trend-following indicator and an oscillating indicator trade a market when it is flat and when it erupts into a trend.

- During a trading channel, you can see the oscillator has a good 'feel' for when the price turns around.
- The moving average on the other hand keeps giving out 'whipsaw' signals.
- Once the market breaks out in a trend however, the oscillator starts giving out less profitable signals.
- In a trending market, the trend-following indicator like the moving average becomes a superior tool. It signals us to open a 'short' trade – marked by the black arrow on the chart – and signals to close the trade at point (x) on the chart. This manages to grab most of the trend.

Fibonacci Numbers

Fibonacci numbers are a sequence of numbers, discovered by Leonardo Pisano Fibonacci. The series begins with: 1, 2, 3, 5, 8, 13, 21, 34, 55, 89, 144, 233, 377 and so on. The last number gets added to the previous number, to make the next number.

The Fibonacci sequence is supposedly recurrent everywhere in nature. The fractions representing the screw-like arrangement of leaves and the number of petals of many flowers are Fibonacci numbers. Buttercups have 5 petals, lilies and iris have 3 petals, some delphiniums have 8, corn marigolds have 13 petals whereas daisies can be found with 34, 55 or even 89 petals. Furthermore, Fibonacci found that, in ideal circumstances, rabbits breed in the same sequence![40]

So if such was the nature of these numbers, traders thought, it might have some significance on trading as well. Coincidentally, there are 5 working days in a week and there are roughly 21 working days in a month. Since people traded in such sequences, it made sense to use it. You would use a 21-day moving average if you wanted to get the average for last month's prices and a 5-day moving average if you wanted to find out last week's average prices.

Technical analysts have imported Fibonacci numbers in their everyday analysis. They often use Fibonacci numbers as the values for their indicator parameters. It is not a requirement that you use them in your trading because they may not be what would work best in a particular timeframe, market or commodity. However, it is useful for traders to recognise them because they are used in a lot of books, trading articles and charting programs.

---

[40] "The Discovery Of The Fibonacci Numbers". Http://www.essaysample.com/essay/002523.html (17th Dec 2005).

Last Note About Indicators

This chapter may not have covered all the available indicators, but having a thorough understanding of these indicators, you can interpret many other indicators because they work in similar ways. When it comes to indicators, I believe that instead of trying to use many, it may be better to choose a few that would suit you. Learn to use them well individually, and learn to use them together with other indicators.

CHAPTER 12: TRADING SYSTEMS

Before getting into the different parts that make up a trading system, I am aware that some readers may have doubts or may not be clear about why they need a trading system. I would like to have a thorough discussion about the need for a trading system because it is important that all readers understand these reasons before anything else.

THE PSYCHOLOGICAL NEED FOR A TRADING SYSTEM

People's psychological struggle is apparent in the markets. You take a look at charts and you can get a feel of how it has been for the people trading that market. The best way for me to explain the psychological difficulty of a person trading without a system is through an example. It is important that I try to be as detailed as I can in what a person may mentally have to go through when executing a trade.

Image 53: Psychological Need For A Trading System

- A novice trader, Bill, decides to trade the USD/JPY 4-hour charts.
- He does not have a trading system. He simply looks at a chart to get a 'gut-feel' for what is going on and then he opens a trade. He has no other rules.
- Let's assume that his position size is $100,000 a trade.
- He has about $10,000 in his account.
- He has a 200:1 margin ratio so he only needs to put up $500 margin to open a trade.
- Trading this size makes him roughly $10 for every point the USD/JPY moves upwards.
- One day, while watching the movements of the USD/JPY, he sees that a support level at 110.45 has just been broken.
- He opens a trade at point (A) when the US is worth 110.45 JPYs.
- He is happy when the market breaks through another resistance level at point (B). At point (B), he already has an unrealised profit of 30 pips or $300.
- When the market gets to point C, he becomes ecstatic. In just two days, he has made $1,200 in profits! He starts to calculate: if the market only performs this good half the time, he will no

doubt, make a million by the end of the year. It is time to get a new car and take that long-awaited holiday.
- Then something happens, the market goes high up and then closes at a price lower than the opening price. He is unaware that other chartists have already identified this as a sign that the market sentiment is about to change.
- In the next four hours, other traders rush to close all their 'long' trades (point D). Some may open downward trades as well. Bill has been watching all this. He regrets not having taken the $1,200 profit while could. He decides to wait for the market to go back up to 111.65 where he is going to take back the profit the market took away from him. He thinks that he has no reason to be scared because he still has a little profit left.
- The market bounces up to point (F). He feels relieved and he expects the market to make a steady climb upward.
- Traders begin selling the USD/JPY again at point (G). Some people, who bought at 110.45, decided to take whatever profits they could. Others simply closed their trades, fearful the market will continue downwards. When the market does go down, Bill will start incurring open losses.
- Bill starts getting worried. Instead of regretting not having taken the $1200 profit, he now regrets not having closed his trade when it was still not losing money. He hopes that if there is a support level, the market might bounce back up so he can close the trade and break-even. It never goes back up though. In fact, people begin selling again.
- When the market reaches 109.60, what had been a $1200 profit is now an $850 loss and it is still counting. He gets angry. Then he feels shame. He cannot get out of a trade like this. His friends, family, and maybe his wife, would laugh at him if they ever find out.
- Bill hesitates in closing his trade. There is a newly-formed support level at 109.60 and an old support just below it. He hopes that when the market bounces on top of any of these two levels, the market will change its direction.
- When the market reaches point (J) on the chart, Bill is suffering a $1,600 loss. It is after this point, that he realises it is better to protect whatever is left of his account rather than hanging on to the USD/JPY.

- If he does not get out of the trade, his loss could only get worse. The pain of losing gets so severe that he has to stop it. Somewhere around point (J), he closes his trade.

It may appear silly for us to aim to buy at high prices and sell at low prices and yet that is what most people end up doing when they begin trading without a system.

What we can learn from this example is that: if you are trading based on gut-feel, hope, fear, greed and make-believe, you will keep making losses. It becomes only a matter time before your account dwindles to an amount that is no longer big enough to open just one contract. Without a system, you are opening yourself up to potential danger.

Consistently-successful people in any endeavour have tested systems that they follow consciously or subconsciously. This allows them to do their tasks efficiently and this increases the odds of success in their favour.

For example, in conducting a sales presentation, a professional salesperson follows a system that guides him away from confusing and agitating a potential customer. An auto mechanic knows the fastest and easiest way to repair an engine. Even in your daily routine, you have a system to do the simplest of tasks. When you wake up and go to work: you may be half-asleep but you consciously know what you have to do. There would be little reason why you should break that routine, because you have already found it to be the most efficient way of getting to work. It is the same with trading. You need a system to trade.

WHAT IS A TRADING SYSTEM?

A trading system is a set of specific rules that will tell you how you should open and exit your trades. You need a system regardless of whether you are using technical or fundamental analysis.

After having learnt about how to use indicators from the last chapter, it may occur to some readers that the indicators have all the rules they need. It is possible to use indicators as stand-alone trading systems; however, do consider that different indicators have their strengths and weaknesses.

For example, trend-following indicators only follow trends. They perform badly when the market is moving sideways. Oscillators do well in flat markets but they do horribly in trending markets. It is also important for a trader to realise that trading is not simply about using indicators. Trading is about understanding your own psychology and exercising safe position-sizing strategies. You need to take all these factors into account and roll up everything you learn in one trading system.

THE REQUIREMENTS OF A TRADING SYSTEM

A trading system has two components:
1. Entering a trade – When and how to open a trade.
2. Exiting a trade – When and how to exit the market.

A trading system must have the following characteristics:

1. Systematic — As a trader, you need to define your trading rules explicitly. The key is to systemise as many of the rules that you have, to make sure that you are clear on what you need to do from the moment you open a trade until you close it. Simplify it in a way so anybody can follow it.

2. Testable — You must be able to test your trading system. If you test the validity of your theories using past data, you can find out if the trading system can profit. You need to isolate each of the variables and each of the assumptions you have made, so you can test them separately.

'Discretionary' Vs 'Mechanical' Rules

Trading systems are made up of a set of rules that could be 'discretionary' or 'mechanical'. Discretionary trading systems contain an unrestricting set of rules which the trader has the flexibility to interpret, use and adjust as he sees fit, depending on market conditions. Mechanical trading systems are trading systems that contain a strict set of rules the trader cannot break, ignore or deviate away from. Both discretionary and mechanical trading systems must continuously be adapted and corrected to keep pace with the changes in the market environment.

The emphasis is placed on whether the set of rules are 'flexible' or 'strict'. It is flexible if the trader is required to interpret or make his own decisions while he is in a trade. It is strict if he is simply required to follow the rules without thinking.

Many profitable traders, who have enough experience and who have learnt to control their emotions, use discretionary trading systems successfully. However, novice traders must ignore whatever they think their intuition or 'gut-feel' is telling them, because these feelings simply have no basis and are often wrong. Novice traders are advised to systemise their rules as soon as possible. This will allow their minds and emotions to intrude less when they are in the middle of their trades. Traders using mechanical trading systems to learn to trade the markets are much like kids using training wheels to learn how to ride bikes.

As you begin trading however, you will probably be using a discretionary trading system. This may not entirely be your choice. You will learn a lot about so many concepts that you would not be able to put all the elements of your system in a fully automatic, mechanical set. You will drown in so much information that, as soon as you think you have your system completed, you find a new idea which requires you to revise your system again. This will happen many times so do not despair.

Eventually, however, you will get to a point where all the bits and pieces of the big puzzle will start to lock together. This will be the early beginning of your mechanical trading system. Continue developing it and trading it until consistent profits begin to show before you start applying discretion to your rules.

Counter-Trend And Trend-Following Systems

In our discussion of 'classical charting' techniques, we have touched on the subject of counter-trend and trend-following trading. We have said that counter-trend trading is a strategy used by people who try to profit from the markets that move sideways. Trend-following strategies try to profit when price breaks into a trend.

Some indicators are designed to catch trends and others trade flat markets. Since trading systems use indicators, they inherit the same qualities. Therefore, in designing a trading system, you must first consider if you mainly want to trade flat markets or whether you would prefer to trade when it erupts into a trend. If you want to be profitable in both, then you have to consider how you may reconcile these differences into your system.

Image 54: Trend Trading & Counter-Trend Trading

In the example above, the market oscillates up and down a trading range. A trading range is also referred to as a trading channel. Counter-trend traders hope to buy at the lows of a channel and sell at the highs of a channel. If they were to have a mantra, it would be: 'buy low then sell high'. Trend-following traders trade when the market breaks out of a channel. If they were to have a mantra it would be to the effect of: 'buy high and sell higher' or 'sell low and buy lower'.

WHEN AND HOW TO ENTER THE MARKET

You can enter the market:
1. When an indicator tells you to, or
2. When your classical charting analysis tells you to.

Once you know when to enter the market, you need to find out how you are going to enter it. There are three main types of orders:

1. Market orders,
2. Stop orders and
3. Limit orders.

Market Orders

Market orders are the simplest orders. Use these to enter the market immediately. Most market orders are executed at the open or at the close of a bar or a candlestick.

Stop Orders

Stop orders are orders that allow you to be in a trade only when the market breaks out from a trading channel. Use these to enter the market only if it continues its direction.

Limit Orders

Limit orders are orders that allow you to be in a trade only when the market gives you a better price than where it is at now. Use these to enter the market when it pulls-back to a 'good' price.

Image 55: Using Stop & Limit Orders

The image above shows you how you may use stop and limit orders. You use a buy limit order if you only want to buy when the market goes down to where you want to enter the market. You use a sell limit order if you want to wait for the market to rise to a certain level you want to sell at. You use a buy stop order if you want to enter a trade when the price erupts upwards. You use a sell stop order if you want to enter a trade when the price erupts downwards.

HOW TO EXIT A TRADE

You can exit a losing trade using many methods including the following:

1. **Indicators** — Exiting a trade by using any technical indicator.

2. **Classical Charting** — Exit trades using trendlines, support-resistance and channels.

3. **Stop-Loss and Take Profit Mechanisms** such as:

    a) **Flat Stop-Loss** — Exit a trade simply after the market goes against you by a certain amount of pips or dollars.

    b) **Flat Take-Profit** — Exit a trade after the market goes against you by a certain amount of pips or dollars.

    c) **Average True Range (ATR) Stop-Loss / Take Profit** — Exiting a trade using a stop-loss that is a factor of the ATR.

    d) **Trailing Stop-Loss / Take Profit** — Exiting a trade by using a trailing stop-loss or a take-profit order. Please note that stop-loss orders are different from buy stop orders and sell stop orders.

    e) **Percent Risk Trailing Stop** — Exit a profitable trade if the market takes back a certain percentage of your open profits.

f) **Break-Even Stop** — Guarantees the trade will not lose money once the market goes a certain distance, measured in pips, in your favour.

Stop-Loss And Take-Profit Mechanisms

It is important to have a stop-loss and a take-profit mechanism incorporated in a trading system. You use a stop-loss mechanism to limit your losses when the market moves against your position. You use a take-profit mechanism to take your profits when the market goes in your direction.

Putting stop-losses too close to your entry points will result in most of your trades being kicked out of a trade. This will make you miss several good trades. Putting stop-losses too far from your entry point makes your losses bigger and thus, damage your profitability.

Using take-profit mechanisms brings the same problem. If you put your take-profit too close to your entry point, you might find that you are missing out on many big profits. If you put it too far, you might find that you are not taking enough of the profits the market is making available to you. Unrealistic profit targets will never get triggered and as a result, big profits become meagre profits or worse, they become losses.

Here are examples of stop-loss and take-profit mechanisms you may add to your system.

a) *Flat Stop-Loss Order*

You may exit a market if it goes against you after a certain number of pips. It is up to you how many pips you think would be suitable. For example, if you are using a stop-loss of 200 pips and you have opened a 'long' trade on the USD/JPY at 114.84, then you need to put a stop-loss at 112.84[41]. This method is the simplest way to exit a losing trade.

---

[41] 114.84 – 2.00 = 112.84

b) Flat Take-Profit Level

You may simply exit a market when it is a profitable trade by a certain number of pips. You may choose to take your profit after the market goes in your direction by say, 250 pips or 400 pips. It is up to you how many pips you think would be suitable. For example, if you are using a take-profit level of 500 pips and you have opened a 'long' trade on the USD/CAD at 1.1722 then you need to put a take-profit level at 1.2222[42]. This method is the simplest way to exit a favourable trade.

c) The ATR-Based Stop-Loss

Instead of just picking a random number, you may want to have a more accurate guess about where you put your stop-loss and your take-profit levels. You can base your stop-loss on something that measures usual market volatility. Created by Mr J. Welles Wilder, the Average True Range (ATR) measures the 'true' price movement of the market from bar to bar. The ATR is the largest value out of the following:

1. The distance from today's high to today's low,
2. The distance from yesterday's close to today's high or
3. The distance from yesterday's close to today's low.

The Average True Range (ATR) is the average of the true ranges over the past x periods (where x is a number specified by the user). The ATR for any x amount of period is calculated easily by several charting and trading platforms, so you do not have to do it yourself.

What you can do is set your stop-loss and take-profit level based on this ATR. You just multiply it by a number or a fraction. For example, the ATR multiplied by 2 would be your stop-loss and the ATR multiplied by 5 would be your take-profit level. The factor that you can use to multiply with the ATR does not necessarily have to be greater than 1 either. It could also be a fraction or a decimal such as 0.75 or 0.50.

---

[42] $1.1722 + 0.0500 = 1.2222$

Let's say that you want to open a 'long' position on the GBP/USD daily charts. The Average True Range over the last 14 days is 146 pips. You have always set your stop-losses at 2 * ATR and your take-profit levels at 5 * ATR. Therefore you need to put your stop-loss 292[43] pips below your entry point. You also need to put a take-profit level of 730[44] pips towards your trade, just in case the market goes in your direction. If you open a 'long' trade at 1.7593, then you need to set your stop-loss level at 1.7301[45] and your take-profit level at 1.8323[46].

You can set this stop-loss at the day of entry to protect you from any adverse movements. You may also use this method as a trailing stop-loss or a trailing take-profit level by recalculating its new value as the trade progresses each bar.

d) *Trailing Stop-Loss / Take-Profit*

This method is called a trailing stop-loss if the trade is losing or a trailing take-profit if the trade is winning. This order is set at the highest high (for 'long' trades) or at the lowest low (for 'short' trades) of the last x numbers of bars.

How to set and use trailing stop-loss and trailing take-profit orders:

For 'long' positions:
1. When entering a trade, set the stop-loss level at the lowest low of the previous bar. You may also want to use the lowest low of the previous 2 bars, 5 bars or 10 bars if you like.
2. As soon as a new bar gets added to your chart, you re-set your stop-loss level to the lowest low of the previous bar.
3. As the market progresses upwards, your stop-loss will come closer and closer to your entry point. Once your stop-loss level becomes greater than your entry-point, it then becomes what is referred to as a trailing take-profit order.

---

[43] 146*2 = 292
[44] 146*5 = 730
[45] 1.7593 − 0.0292 = 1.7301
[46] 1.7593 + 0.0730 = 1.8323

For 'short' positions,
1. When entering a trade, set the stop-loss level at the highest high of the previous bar. You may also want to use the highest high of the previous 2 bars, 5 bars or 10 bars.
2. As soon as a new bar gets added to your chart, you reset your stop-loss level to the highest high of the previous bar.
3. As the market progresses downwards, your stop-loss will come closer and closer to your entry point. Once your stop-loss level becomes less than your entry-point, it then becomes what is referred to as a trailing take-profit order.

Below is a graphical example of what happens.

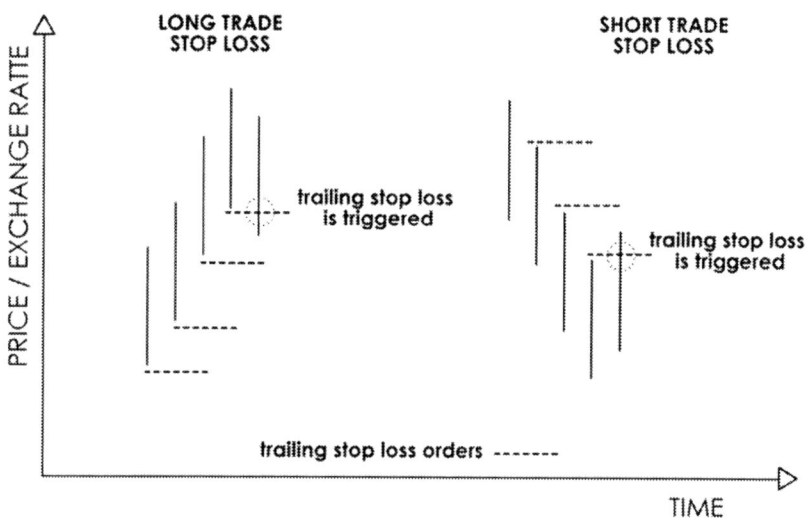

Image 56: Stop-Loss Set At The Extreme Levels Of 1 Bar Ago

- You put a 'long' stop-loss order at the low of the preceding bar. Do this every time a new bar is added on the chart, until a stop-loss gets triggered by the price that crosses it.
- You put a 'short' stop-loss order at the high of the preceding bar. This is done every time a new bar is added on the chart until a stop-loss order gets triggered by the price crossing it.

In the example below, the stop-loss orders for the 'long' trade are placed at the lowest low of the last 5 days. The stop-loss orders for the 'short' trades are placed at the highest high of the last 5 days.

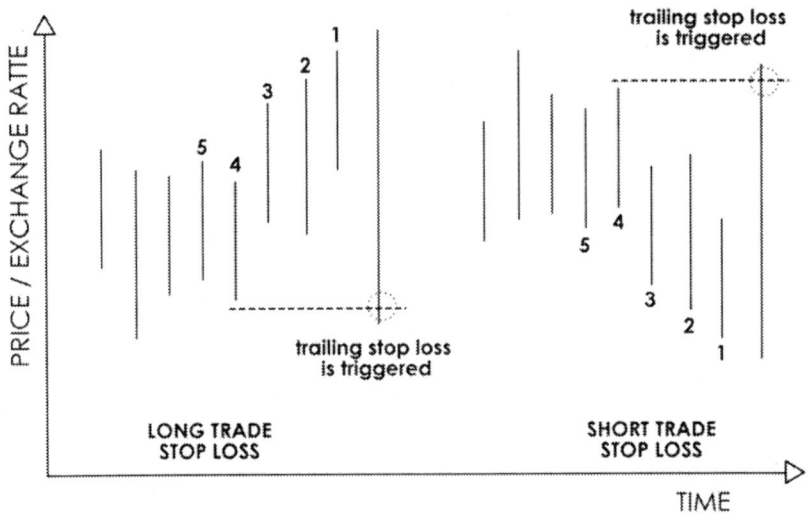

Image 57: Stop-Loss Set At The Extreme Levels Of 5 Bars Ago

e) 'Percent Risk Trailing' Take-Profit

This exit strategy only applies when you have a profitable trade. The idea is to protect a certain percentage of your open profit just in case the market starts pulling back against your direction. For example, if you have a 'long' position and the market goes 200 pips in your favour, you may decide to put a stop-loss 100 pips above where you bought. This ensures that you keep 50%[47] of your profit if the market drops down by 100 pips.

To make this work, you need a minimum amount that when reached, will activate this strategy. We will refer to this amount as the 'minimum activation amount'. In this case, this number is 200 pips. You then need to decide what percentage of your open profits you want to keep. In this case, it is 50%.

Please note that if the price never goes above the 'minimum activation amount of 200 pips above the entry point, this strategy will not get triggered. Some brokers have this take-profit order built into their trading platforms. With other brokers, you may have to do it manually.

---

[47] 100 points / 200 points = 0.50

f) 'Break-Even' Stop-Loss

This exit strategy only applies when the market goes in your favour by a certain distance, measured in pips. The idea is to avoid a loss once the trade becomes profitable. Much like the 'Percent Risk Trailing Take Profit' strategy, you need a minimum amount that when reached, will activate this strategy. We will refer to this amount as the 'minimum activation amount'. For instance, you could set this to be 150 pips so that, as soon as the price hits 150 pips above your entry price, you move your stop-loss level to your entry price. If the market changes direction, you will not lose money. However, if the price never reaches 150 pips above your entry price, this strategy will not activate.

ASSEMBLING YOUR TRADING SYSTEM

In this chapter and the chapter on classical charting and technical indicators, you may have learnt enough strategies to start assembling bits and pieces into one trading system. Before you begin, I suggest the following:

1. You use a signal from an indicator or a 'classsical charting' technique to enter a trade.
2. You decide what type of order you will use to enter the market,
3. You use a signal from an indicator or from a classical charting technique to close the trade.
4. You have a stop-loss placement strategy just in case the market goes against you,
5. You have a take-profit placement strategy just in case the market goes in your favour.

To summarise all the possible components you can use, I have put them in the table below.

Table 1: Trading System Components

Entry Strategy	Order	Exit Strategy	Stop-Loss Exits	Take-Profit Exits
Trendlines	Market Order	Trendlines	None	None
S-R Levels	Stop Order	S-R Levels	Flat	Flat
Trend Channels	Limit Order	Trend Channels	ATR	ATR
Moving Average		Moving Average	Trailing	Trailing
MACD		MACD	Break-even	Percent Risk Trailing
Stochastic Oscillators		Stochastic Oscillators		
Williams'%R		Williams'%R		
CCI		CCI		
Total: 8	Total: 3	Total: 8	Total: 5	Total: 5
Total of 4800[48] Combinations!				

Looking at the table above, you can have up to 4800 different ways of putting together a system based on all the tactics you have learnt from this book so far. You may apply rules to filter your entry and exit signals.

An example of a filtering rule could be that you take action on the buy signals of the moving average only if the Stochastic Oscillator gives you a buy signal too. In such an example, you have one layer of filter. The moving average would be your leading signal and the Stochastic Oscillator is your filtering signal.

You may also decide to have two layers of filters. For example, you take action on the buy signals of the moving average only if the Stochastic Oscillator and the CCI give you a buy signal.

The effect of adding filters will greatly impact on the number of different ways you can design your system. The table

---

[48] $8 * 3 * 8 * 5 * 5 = 4800$

below shows what happens if we add only one layer of filter for the entry signals and one layer of filter for the exit signals.

Entry Strategy		Order	Exit Strategy		SL	TP
Lead	Filter		Lead	Filter	Exits	Exits
TL	TL	MO	TL	TL	None	None
SR	SR	StO	SR	SR	Flat	Flat
TC	TC	LO	TC	TC	ATR	ATR
MA	MA		MA	MA	TR	TR
MACD	MACD		MACD	MACD	BE	%RT
SO	SO		SO	SO		
W%R	W%R		W%R	W%R		
CCI	CCI		CCI	CCI		
Σ: 8	Σ: 7[49]	Σ: 3	Σ: 8	Σ: 7[50]	Σ: 5	Σ: 5

Abbreviations:

Σ = Total
%RT = Percentage Risk Trailing
BE = Break Even
CCI = Commodity Channel Index
LO = Limit Order
MA = Moving Average
MACD = Moving Average Convergence Divergence
MO = Market Order
SO = Stochastic Oscillator

SR = Support-Resistance
SL = Stop Loss
StO = Stop Order
TC = Trend Channel

TL = Trendline
TP = Take-Profit
TR = Trailing

W%R = Williams'%R

Total of 235,200[51] combinations!

Two-hundred, thirty-five thousand, two-hundred different combinations: that is astounding! To find the optimal combination to trade the market and the instrument you are trying to trade, you would have to perform at least that many tests. I have not even considered many of the other technical indicators available and each one has its own set of variables that you can vary. That is a lot of testing, but all you need to do is to find one of those

---

[49] 8 signals – 1 signal = 7. The reason why we only have 7 available filtering signals left is because once you have used one signal as your leading indicator, then you cannot use that same one to be your filtering signal.
[50] Ibid.
[51] 8 * 7 * 3 * 8 * 7 * 5 * 5 = 235200.

combinations competent enough to give you a positive mathematical 'edge' to make money.

If you do not have a working system, you will fail regardless of how good your risk-management strategy is, or how disciplined you may be. Finding a system that works is going to be one of the hardest and the longest stages of your journey.

EXAMPLES OF TRADING SYSTEMS

In our discussions of 'classical charting' techniques and indicators, I have provided you with plenty of examples that may joggle your mind with a couple of potential trading systems. I am going to provide you with three more examples of systems based on the information we have covered so far. Please note that I have chosen ideal situations to highlight what the system is trying to do. There is little chance that any of these systems would be profitable the way they are without much tweaking and modification to suit the market and the instrument that you would be trading. The purpose of this exercise is to give you an idea on how you can combine the different parts of technical analysis to make a trading system.

IMPORTANT:
Trading the financial markets is risky. The trading systems provided are for illustrative purposes only. The author does not guarantee that any of the trading systems provided in this book are profitable.

Let us start off with a simple one.

THE EXPLOSIVE TRADING SYSTEM

This system is an example of a break-out system: a system that tries to profit from those moments when the market erupts from a trading channel to a trend.

THE TOOLS YOU NEED:
    1. **Support-Resistance levels** — To mark your entries.

2. **Moving-average** — To trigger your exits.
3. **Stop Order** — To ensure that you only get into a trade if the market continues in your direction.
4. **Stop-Loss** — Two support levels under the entry point.
5. **Take Profit** — We assume none for this example.

THE RULES FOR A 'LONG' TRADE
1. Wait for the market to start oscillating between a trading range. Start marking support-resistance levels on the chart, where the price could potentially break out.
2. Put buy stop orders 10 pips above resistance levels and put sell stop orders 10 pips below support levels.
3. As soon as you are in a trade, place a stop-loss order two support levels below the entry point.
4. Wait for the moving average to trigger your exit point.
5. Remove the unexecuted sell stop order.

THE RULES FOR A 'SHORT' TRADE
1. Wait for the market to start oscillating between a trading range. Start marking support-resistance levels on the chart, where the price could potentially break out.
2. Put buy stop orders 10 pips below resistance levels and put sell stop orders 10 pips below support levels.
3. As soon as you are in a trade, place a stop-loss order two resistance levels above the entry point.
4. Wait for the moving average to trigger your exit point.
5. Remove the unexecuted sell stop order.

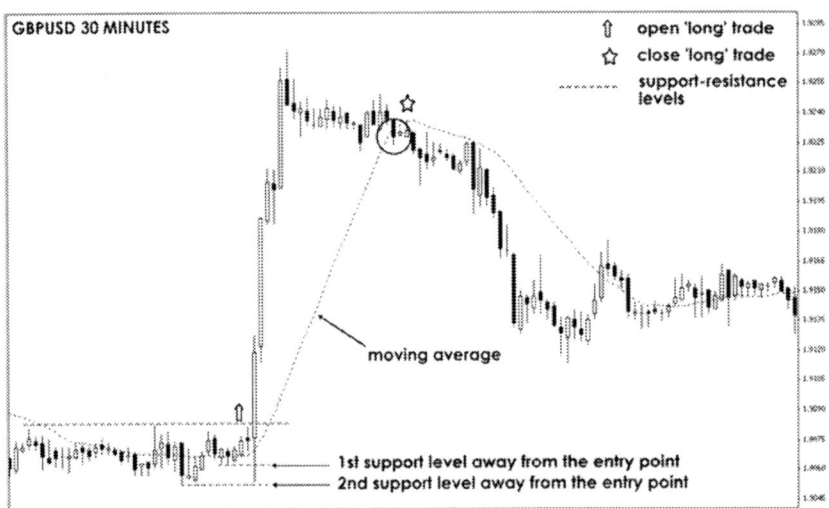

Image 58: The Explosive Trading System In Action

The chart above is an example of what types of trades a system like this could have executed:

- At the start of the chart, we see a resistance level.
- We set a buy stop order ten pips above that resistance level to minimise the chances of the signals being triggered by a false breakout above that resistance level.
- After a breakout occurs, we get into a trade. On the chart, you can see our entry point close to the white arrow.
- We set a stop-loss level, 5 pips below the second support level underneath our entry level. Note that if we did place our stop-loss only 1 support level under our entry point, we would have been kicked out of this good trade. This is why it is important to test your systems to make sure that most of the time, your stop-loss levels are not too close to your entry points.
- In this example, the trade is a success and all the trader has to do is to wait for the price to close under the moving-average to close the trade.
- The white star on the chart marks where we would have taken our profit.

THE HALF-A-SLICE TRADING SYSTEM

Moving averages identify trends well and they give us good signals to let us know when a trend has changed. We can use these signals to open a trade towards a new trend. The problem is that if we rely on the same moving average to give us a signal to close the trade, it might already be too late. By the time we get the signal, the market would have lost most of its momentum and may have already taken back most of our open profits.

We know that a moving average with a long timeframe gives a more delayed signal but it is likely to give us 'whipsaw' signals. A moving average with a short timeframe gives us more whipsaws but it is also more sensitive to any change in market direction. We would then speculate that we may have a workable system if we open a trade based on a longer moving average to avoid many whipsaw signals. After that, we can use a shorter moving average to warn us early when the market begins to change direction.

THE TOOLS NEEDED:

1. **Long-term moving average** — Signals your entry.
2. **Short-term moving average** — Signals your exit.
3. **Market Order**
4. **Stop-Loss** — Optional*.
5. **Take Profit** — Optional*.

* You may want to add a stop-loss and take-profit orders. We will not assume any stop-loss and take-profit signals to simplify this example.

THE RULES FOR A 'LONG' TRADE

1. Wait for the price to close above the long-term moving average. This will be your signal to open a 'long' trade.
2. You open the trade at the close of the bar using a Market Order.

3. Wait for the price to close under the short-term moving average. This will be your signal to close your 'long' trade.
4. You close the trade at the close of the bar using a Market Order.

THE RULES FOR A 'SHORT' TRADE

1. Wait for the price to close under the long-term moving average. This will be your signal to open a 'short' trade.
2. You open the trade at the close of the bar using a Market Order.
3. Wait for the price to close above the short-term moving average. This will be your signal to close your 'short' trade.
4. You close the trade at the close of the bar using a Market Order.

Below is an example of how this system might catch a trade.

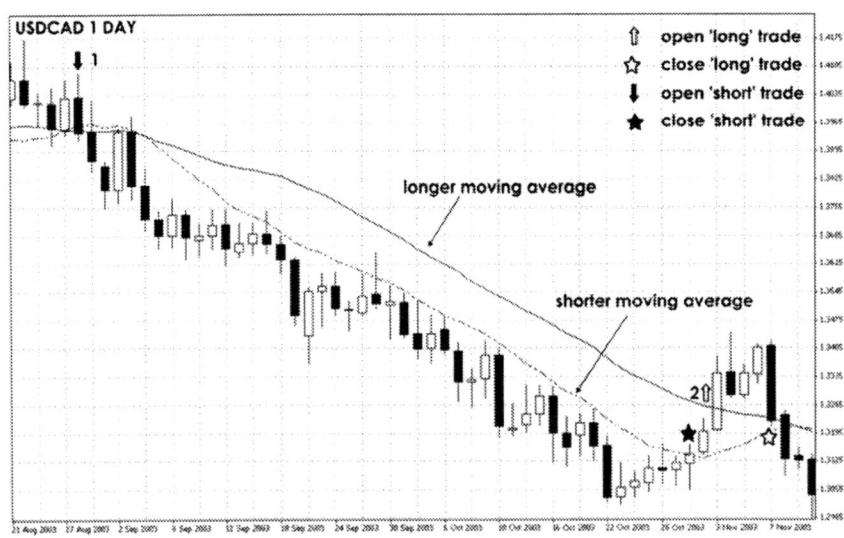

Image 59: The Half-A-Slice Trading System In Action

- We begin by opening Trade 1 since the price closed under the longer moving average.

- We wait until the price closes above the shorter moving average. This is marked by the black star on the chart.
- We open Trade 2 after the price closes above the longer moving average and then we close the trade when the price closes under the shorter moving average. This is indicated by the white star on the chart.

Out of the two trades, only one is profitable. We hope the gains we make from trades like the first trade would be enough to cover for the losses we incur from trades like the second one. The only way to find out with some degree of certainty is by testing this system.

THE SHOGUN TRADING SYSTEM

Let me show you a slightly different trading system that uses an indicator to filter the signals of a leading indicator. This system is similar to what I used in my early days to trade the 4-hour charts of certain currency pairs.

We must first identify the trend of the market. By identifying the trend, we can ignore half of the information the market is giving us. For example, if we identify a bullish trend, we are then able ignore all opportunities to trade downwards. This will make it easier for us to focus. We will use the MACD to tell us if we have a 'bullish' trend or a 'bearish' trend. If the MACD Histogram and its moving average intersect, it means the current trend is weakening and we start looking for a trade against the weakened trend.

After we identify which direction to trade towards, we will use an oscillator like the Stochastic Oscillator to time our entries and our exits. Therefore, the MACD is the leading indicator and the Stochastic is a filtering indicator: it filters the signals given by the MACD. Here are two diagrams that will show us how we will be using the Stochastic.

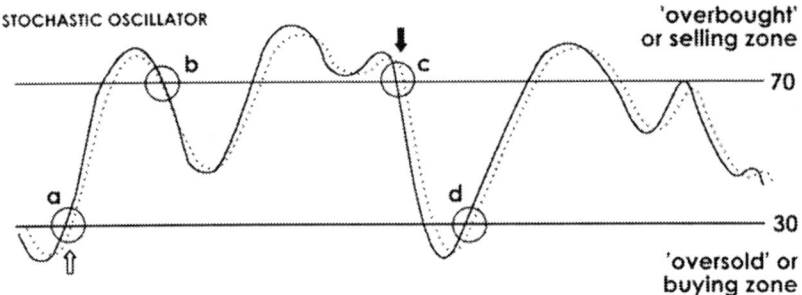

Image 60: Trade Signals For The Shogun Trading System

When the Stochastic crosses above 30, marked (a) on the chart, we open a 'long' trade. As soon as it goes over the selling zone and makes a U-turn downwards, crossing under the 70 level, we close the trade. If the oscillator does not make it over the selling zone, then we will just assume the trade will not be profitable so we close it. We need to specify exactly how we are going to exit a trade when this happens. If we are in a 'long' trade that goes 'bad', we exit when the Stochastic Oscillator starts behaving as it does in events (a), (b) and (c), on the diagram below.

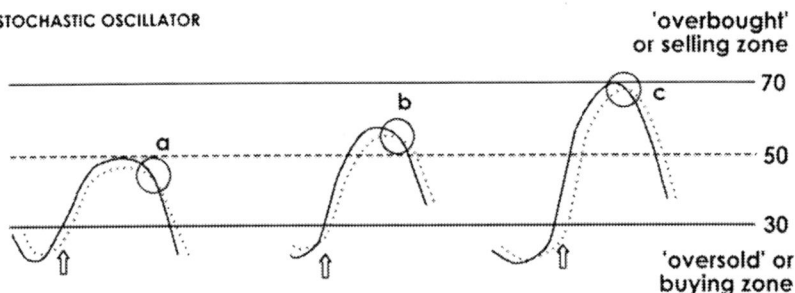

Image 61: Stochastic Signals That The Current 'Long' Trend Is Weak

We open 'short' trades when the Stochastic crosses under level 70 from the selling zone (point c, Image 60). We wait until it goes to the buying zone. We close the trade when it crosses above level 30 (point d, Image 60). If we are in a 'short' trade that goes 'bad', we exit when the Stochastic starts behaving as it does in events (a), (b) and (c), on the chart below.

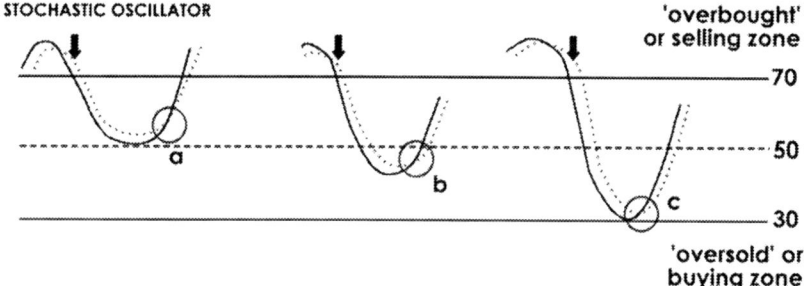

Image 62: Stochastic Signals That 'Short' Trade Signal Is Weak

We have built-in exit strategies within the Stochastic Oscillator that tells us when to close our good and bad trades. Therefore we are not going to add any more stop-loss or take-profit strategies to this system.

THE TOOLS YOU NEED

1. **MACD (Settings: 12,26,9)** – To read the trend.
2. **Stochastic Oscillator (Settings: 14,5,5)** – To time our entries and exits.
3. **Stop Order** – Order at the high or the low of the bar when the signal has occurred.
4. **Stop-Loss** – None.*
5. **Take Profit** – None.*

* The Stochastic Oscillator has enough exit strategies just in case the market goes against us.

THE RULES FOR A 'LONG' TRADE

1. If the MACD Histogram is greater than the MACD Histogram Moving Average, then we assume the trend is 'bullish'.
2. We will look out for when the Stochastic Oscillator presents us with a buy signal. When it does, we put an order at the high of the signal bar, just to make sure that we are in the market only if it continues to go upwards.

3. As soon as we open a 'long' trade, we wait for the signal of the Stochastic to tell us when to close the trade.

THE RULES FOR A 'SHORT' TRADE

1. If the MACD Histogram is less than the MACD Histogram Moving Average, then we assume the trend is 'bearish'.
2. We will look for when the Stochastic Oscillator presents us with a sell signal. When it does, we put an order at the low of the signal bar, just to make sure that we are in the market only if the market continues to go downwards.
3. As soon as we open a 'short' trade, we wait for the signal of the Stochastic to tell us when to close the trade.

Here are sample trades for this system.

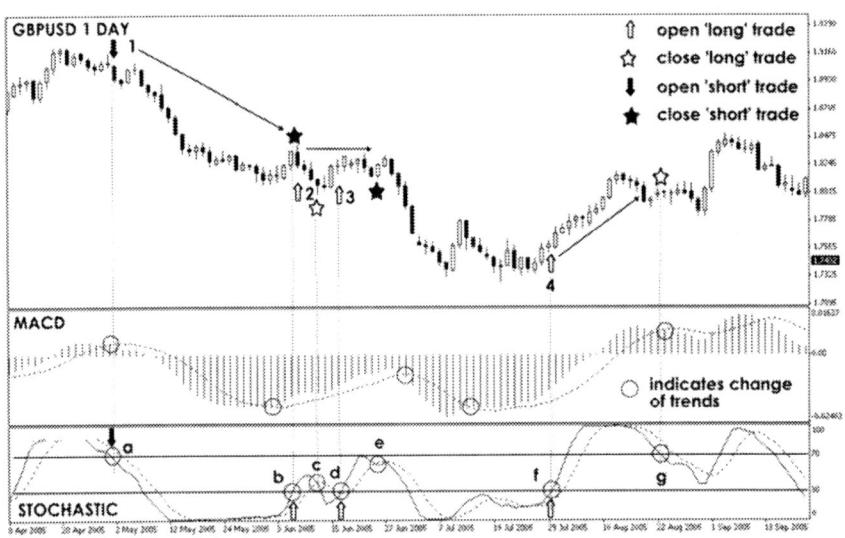

Image 63: The Shogun Trading System In Action

Consider the example above:
- The MACD signals the 'bullish' trend is about to turn 'bearish'.
- After that, the Stochastic makes a signal for us to open a 'short' trade, marked (a) on the chart.

- The trade continues until the Stochastic signals for us to close it. This signal is marked (b) on the Stochastic.
- By this time, the MACD already shows a 'bullish' trend. The Stochastic gives us a buy signal and so we open trade number 2. This signal is marked (b) on the chart. It is the same signal to close the previous trade.
- The market is not going to go up and this is detected by the Stochastic to close the losing trade at point (c).
- The Stochastic signals for us to buy again at the signal marked (d) on the chart.
- At point (e), we get a signal from the Stochastic to close the trade because the market is not likely to go upwards.
- The MACD signals a change of trend twice after this before the Stochastic gives us the fourth buy signal, marked (f) on the chart.
- We close this trade at a profit when the Stochastic signals for us to close the trade at point (g).

Overall, we made two good trades and two losing trades where we lost a small amount. We hope that when we trade this system, the gains we get from the likes of the first and the fourth trade would cover more than the losses we make from the likes of the second and the third trade. The only way we are going to find this out is by testing our system, which I will cover in the next chapter.

SIMPLIFY YOUR SYSTEMS

Whenever you have the chance to simplify your trading system, do so. The simpler it is, the easier it is to test and the less complicated it will be for you to follow. Most importantly, the more variables you add to your trading system, the less flexible it will become. Rigid systems are less likely to be profitable in the future. This is because of the concepts of optimisation and 'curve-fitting'.

OPTIMISATION AND CURVE FITTING

Optimisation is the process of adjusting a trading system to try to make it more effective. These types of adjustments may include changing, adding or removing indicators or their parameters. Optimisation is necessary to get the most out of a system but it may unintentionally lead to the practice of 'curve-fitting'.

'Curve-fitting' is the result of over-optimisation that allows the testing results of a trading system to look phenomenal. However, when the trading system is used to trade real market conditions, it falls apart because its parameters are only set to deal with the market conditions of the past. If you see a system that gives very optimistic results, beware. The system is probably 'curve-fitted' to suit the test data.

WHAT IS NEXT?

In this chapter, we have discussed the different components that make up a trading system. We have talked about entry signals, market orders, exit signals, stop-loss strategies as well as profit-taking strategies. I have provided three trading systems to illustrate how you as a trader may design yours. The next step is to try to get an idea of how well your system might survive the future.

CHAPTER 13: TESTING TRADING SYSTEMS

When you have a trading system, it is dangerous to assume that it will be profitable just because you base it on ideas you believe to be rational. After you have developed a system, your task is not to behave as if you have found the 'holy grail' of all systems and that you must protect and defend it with determination. What you must do, is to behave exactly the opposite way. Detach its value from your self-worth. Forget that it has been the result of your hard work and brilliant thinking.

Identify the assumptions you made deliberately including any that you may have made unknowingly. Ask yourself if your assumptions make sense. Be diligent in finding their weaknesses and hone in on those if you find any. Your task now is to convince yourself that you have a robust system. There is no other way to do this than to test it rigorously in every possible way that you can think of.

USING PAST DATA

How exactly are we going to test our systems? We test our systems by applying it to the market conditions of the past by using past price data. There has been some confusion about this and some people might say: '…yes but the past will never be like the future, what would be the use in using past data to trade?' Let me explain.

Consider that you bought a dog for the first time and you want to take it out for a walk in the park. You have a long leash. You tie one end to the dog's collar and you hold on to the other end. The question is: how much leash do you give him? You give him only a metre of leash on the first day. You realise the dog requires more for him to move around and enjoy the walk. The next day you give him fifteen metres of leash and you find the dog running around, tying the leash around bushes and so on. Imagine doing this everyday for a month or two. Eventually you come to realise that 80% of the time, the dog only needs between 5 to 7 metres of leash to enjoy the walks without tying himself around obstacles. After finding this out, what are you likely to do the next day? You will most likely give the dog somewhere between 5 to 7 metres of rope because there is an 80% chance that you are right. After a couple of months, you begin to get an idea of what your dog is likely to do and what not.

My point is that, even though the past behaviour of the dog will not exactly be the same in the future, you have a very good indication of what your expectations should be after studying his past behaviour. Overnight, your dog will not shrink to the size of a mouse or inflate to the size of an elephant, so you still have an excellent chance that the next day, you can get by with a leash that is only 5 to 7 metres in length. The same inference can be made of the market.

Let us assume that you have a system that uses only a 30-bar moving average to trade the USD/JPY. You open a 'long' trade if the market closes above the moving average and you trade 'short' if it closes under the moving average. You test that theory over the past say, fifteen years and you find that it would have traded 1000 times. If in 60% of those cases, it profited twice as much as it lost the other 40%, then that is a significant statistical advantage. Unless you are testing your system wrongly or on faulty data, there is a high probability that your system will make money.

I hope the analogy of the dog and the trading example I have provided above exemplifies the point I am trying to make about the statistical validity of using past data to trade the market in the future.

THE MEANS OF TESTING YOUR SYSTEM

There are several ways to test your system:
1. Pay someone else to do it for you,
2. Use a computer program designed specifically to test trading systems,
3. You use a spreadsheet program like Microsoft Excel,
4. Manually and
5. Paper-trading.

Paying Someone Else

Computer programmers can test your trading systems for you by offering specialised services. You can tell them how you want to conduct the tests, and of course, they will tell you how much they are going to charge you for it. Depending on the knowledge and experience of the programmer or programmers doing the testing, they could do a thorough assessment of the robustness of your system. They may even suggest ideas about how to improve it. Their expertise would speed up your learning.

Using Technical Analysis Software

Most of us would probably just opt to do the testing ourselves. Doing it yourself will give you insight in constructing trading systems and how to improve the quality of your next one. A few charting programs can test your systems automatically. The challenge for you would be to learn the computer language those programs use so you can command them to conduct the tests the way you want. It can be time-consuming but, then again, all methods of testing trading systems are time-consuming.

Testing Using Spreadsheet Programs

You may use a spreadsheet program to test your ideas. All you need to work with are the opens, closes, highs and lows of the exchange rate of the currency pair you want to trade. Your broker will most likely provide this data. Some brokers though, depending on their trading platform, may not allow you to get access to the price data their charting program uses because of their company policy or technical constraints.

There are many sources of data and their quality and costs are just as varied. If you would like to get some access to free data to play around with initially, you can log on to www.marquezcomelab.com, where I keep a list of places where you can get access to free financial data.

With this method of testing, you will have to develop a knack in using your spreadsheet program. It will come with practice. The most popular spreadsheet program so far is *Microsoft Excel* and it is accessible for everybody. Almost every computer sold nowadays has it preinstalled. Even most public libraries provide you with computers that have *Microsoft Excel*. It is a cost-effective way to test your ideas. You would probably want to simplify your trading systems to make it easier for you to test them. It can get confusing when you have to use a spreadsheet to calculate the moving average of the moving average of the difference between two different moving averages[52], if you get my drift.

Testing Manually

People may prefer to test their systems manually because of the following reasons:

- They are not sure whether they should invest the money in a program that might be hard to learn or that may not be suited for them,

---

[52] The derivation of the moving average of a MACD Histogram.

- Their system rules are so complex that it is difficult to code into a computer or
- They may have a discretionary trading system that requires their analysis and input in executing the system.

Testing manually is nothing more complicated than a trader putting a ruler on top of the charts, going over the data bar-by-bar to simulate what they would have done had they been trading the market in the past.

Manually testing discretionary trading systems, gives traders a way to test their theories; however, this method may hamper the objectivity of the tests. The individuals conducting these tests will be looking at the trades with the benefit of hindsight. It is tempting to lift the ruler and see which direction the market may have gone. How they think they would have traded the market is influenced by their bias since they already know what the market does subsequently.

This is why a trading system must be simple. Most of its rules should be mechanised as much as possible. This will minimise the need for the trader's judgment in interpreting the rules.

Paper Trading

If you base your system on technical analysis, you can choose to test it on past data manually, or by using a system-tester or a spreadsheet. After that, you may choose to use paper-trading as the final step in your attempt to scrutinise the validity of your system.

Most brokers have 'play' accounts that simulate market action, allowing you to speculate what you are going to do when you trade with real money. Paper trading could be the only testing method available for certain traders. I imagine that this would be the only way to test most trading systems that are based on fundamental analysis[53].

---

[53] This is because fundamental analysis takes into account a lot of different information from many sources that could be hard or impossible to obtain. They work with theoretical models that attempt to replicate the different components

HOW TO CONDUCT YOUR EXPERIMENTS

If you have decided that you are not going to pay someone else to test your system, let us advance to the process of how you may conduct your own experiments.

The process of testing your system includes the following steps:

1. Gather the 'trade data' of your system,
2. Calculate the statistical parameters of your system, and
3. Assess the validity of your system

Gather The 'Trade Data' Of Your System

What we want to gather in this exercise is the trade-by-trade data which would have been the result of trading your system. To do this, you need to apply your trading system to the past data of the currency pair you would like to trade. If you want to trade the daily chart of the USD/JPY then you need to have the record of its opening price, its highest price, lowest price and its daily closing price. If you have a system-testing application, you can produce your trade-by-trade data automatically.

For those of you doing the tests manually, the steps outlined below show how you can get your trade records:

1) You need to run your tools on the chart you wish to trade: draw your lines and plot the indicators you will be using,
2) Find out where on the chart you would have opened a trade,
3) Write down the date and the time of when you would have opened this trade,
4) Take note if it is a 'long' trade or a 'short' trade,

---

of the real world. Therefore, in most cases, the only laboratory they can test their ideas on is that of the real-world.

5) Write down the price level where you would have entered the market,
6) Find out where you would have closed that trade,
7) Write down the price where you would have exited the market,
8) Write down the date and the time of when you would have closed the trade,
9) Calculate the profit you would have made in pips and
10) Calculate the profit you would have made in dollars.

We need to write down the date and time of our entries and exits because if we stuff up somewhere in our testing, we can always go back to those dates to check our figures. In doing this exercise, it is important to keep your objectivity as much as possible and stop yourself from cheating.

When you calculate how much money you would have gained or lost, you need to assume that you are trading only a fixed-size contract. For example, for the entire duration of the experiment or for all your experiments from now on, assume that you are only trading 10,000 or 100,000 units of a currency. This way you can have uniformity with all the other experiments you will be conducting. This will allow you to make fair comparisons later. Here is how you may want to lay out your spreadsheet to keep a record of these numbers.

ENTRY DATE & TIME	TRADE TYPE: LONG OR SHORT	ENTRY PRICE	EXIT PRICE	EXIT DATE & TIME	PROFIT OR LOSS IN POINTS	PROFIT OR LOSS IN DOLLARS

Image 64: Experiment Data Layout

Sample Size And How Much Data You Need

Each trade that your system executes in your test is a sample trade. If you only had access to one year data and your system traded 10 times for that year, then you have a sample size of 10. If you have a system that traded 20 times that year, then your sample size is 20. The aim is to maximise your sample size so you are able to derive conclusions with some statistical certainty. The more sample size you have, the more accurate your tests will reflect the true nature of the market.

To illustrate this, consider the case of a coin-toss. There is a 50% chance that it lands on its head and there is another 50% chance that it will land on its tail. If you toss a coin four times, it may come up as heads three times and tails only once. In this example, you have a sample size of 4 and the experiment shows there is a 75% chance that heads come up and 25% chance that tails come up. This is contrary to what we know to be a fact: a fact there is a 50-50 chance between the heads and the tails showing up.

The problem with this test is that the sample size is too small. What you need to do is to toss the coin some more to increase your sample size. You will eventually prove that the more coin tosses you make, the more obvious the fifty-fifty ratio will become. Mathematicians would say: as your sample size approaches infinity, your certainty approaches a factor of one[54].

Therefore, the amount of data you would need would depend on how often your trading system gives out signals to open and close trades. Personally, I look for enough data to allow my system to make 100 trades. Of course if you have a system that trades only twice a year, and you only have 5 years of data to test on, then you may just have to make do with a sample size of 10. Be aware though that the results of your tests may not be an accurate representation of how your system would fare in real life.

Calculate The Statistical Parameters Of Your System

Exactly, what statistical parameters are we talking about? The next table shows an extensive list of what you need to find out about your system.

---

[54] 0 means no probability, 1 means 100% probability.

Trading Parameters	
Initial Account Equity	
Profit Summary	
Total Net Profit	Highest Closed Trade Equity
Gross Profit	Lowest Closed Trade Equity
Gross Loss	Final Account Equity
Profit Factor	Return on Starting Equity
Trades Results	
Number of Trades	Number of Winning Trades
Percent Profitable	Number of Losing Trades
Largest Winning Trade ($)	Largest Losing Trade ($)
Largest Winning Trade (%)	Largest Losing Trade (%)
Average Winning Trade ($)	Average Losing Trade ($)
Average Winning Trade (%)	Average Losing Trade (%)
Maximum Number of Consecutive Wins	Maximum Number of Consecutive Losses
Average Trade ($)	Win/Loss Ratio ($/$)
Average Trade (%)	Win/Loss Ratio (%/%)
Trade Standard Deviation($)	Return/Drawdown Ratio
Trade Standard Deviation(%)	Modified Sharpe Ratio
Drawdowns	
Number of Closed Trade Drawdowns	Worst Case Drawdown
Average Drawdown ($)	Trade Number at Trough
Average Drawdown (%)	Number of Trades in Drawdown
Average Number of Trades in Drawdowns	Worst Case Drawdowns (%)

At the time of writing, I use a program written and distributed by Adaptrade Software which automatically calculates the items above. (Their website URL is http://www.adaptrade.com.)

With the blessing of the people from Adaptrade Software, I provide you with the list of what these items mean:

TRADING PARAMETERS
- **Initial Account Equity**: The starting account size in dollars.

PROFIT SUMMARY:
- **Gross Profit**: The sum of the winning trades
- **Gross Loss**: The sum of the losing trades
- **Total Net Profit**: Gross profit plus gross loss (where gross loss is a negative number).
- **Profit Factor**: Gross profit divided by the absolute value of gross loss. Profit factors of 1.5 or more suggest a strong system. A trading system or method with a low profit factor could become unprofitable with just a slight change in market dynamics.
- **Highest Closed Trade Equity**: The greatest value of account equity on a closed trade basis over all trades in the current sequence.
- **Lowest Closed Trade Equity**: The lowest value of account equity on a closed trade basis over all trades in the current sequence.
- **Final Account Equity**: Value of account equity on the last trade.
- **Return on Starting Equity**: Percentage change in account equity from the first to the last trade relative to the initial account equity.

TRADE RESULTS

- **Number of Trades**: Total number of trades, excluding those with zero number of contracts.
- **Number of Winning Trades**: Total number of trades with a profit/loss greater than zero.
- **Number of Losing Trades**: Total number of trades with a profit/loss less than or equal to zero.
- **Percent Profitable**: The winning trades expressed as a percentage of the total number of trades.

- **Largest Winning Trade ($)**: Largest winning trade, where the winners are expressed in dollars. Largest Winning Trade (%): Largest winning trade, where each winner is expressed as a percentage of account equity at the time the trade was made.
- **Average Winning Trade ($)**: Average of the winning trades, where the winners are expressed in dollars.
- **Average Winning Trade (%)**: Average of the winning trades, where each winner is expressed as a percentage of account equity at the time the trade was made.
- **Max Number Consecutive Wins**: Largest number of winning trades in a row.
- **Largest Losing Trade ($)**: Largest losing trade, where the losses are expressed in dollars.
- **Largest Losing Trade (%)**: Largest losing trade, where each loss is expressed as a percentage of account equity at the time the trade was made.
- **Average Losing Trade ($)**: Average of the losing trades, where the losses are expressed in dollars.
- **Average Losing Trade (%)**: Average of the losing trades, where each loss is expressed as a percentage of account equity at the time the trade was made.
- **Max Number Consecutive Losses**: Largest number of losing trades in a row.
- **Average Trade ($)**: Average of all trades, where the trades are expressed in dollars.
- **Average Trade (%)**: Average of all trades, where each trade is expressed as a percentage of account equity at the time the trade was made.
- **Trade Standard Deviation ($)**: Standard deviation of the trades, where the trades are expressed in dollars. The standard deviation is a measure of variability or dispersion. 68% of normally distributed values are within one standard deviation of the average. 99.7% are within three standard deviations of the average.
- **Trade Standard Deviation (%)**: Standard deviation of the trades, where each trade is expressed as a percentage of account equity at the time the trade was made.
- **Win/Loss Ratio ($ / $)**: Ratio of average winning trade to average losing trade, where the trades are expressed in dollars.

- **Win/Loss Ratio (% / %)**: Ratio of average winning trade to average losing trade, where each trade is expressed as a percentage of account equity at the time the trade was made.
- **Return/Drawdown Ratio**: Return on starting equity divided by the maximum percentage peak-to-valley closed trade drawdown.
- **Modified Sharpe Ratio**: Sharpe Ratio[55] = (ROR − RFI) / STDEV
    Where:
    ROR = Your system's rate of return
    RFI = the risk-free rate of return (usually T-Bills)
    STDEV = the standard deviation of your system's return

DRAWDOWNS

A drawdown is defined as a decline from the highest prior peak of the trader's trading account to its lowest trough.

- **Number of Closed Trade Drawdowns**: This is the total number of drawdowns over the current sequence of trades.
- **Average Drawdown ($)**: Average value of the drawdowns expressed in dollars.
- **Average Drawdown (%)**: Average value of the drawdowns expressed as percentage declines from the prior highest peak in equity.
- **Average Number of Trades in Drawdowns**: Average number of trades from the start of a drawdown until the first trade that makes a new equity high.
- **Worst-case Drawdown ($)**: Largest drawdown, where the drawdowns are expressed in dollars.
- **Trade Number at Trough**: The number of the trade at the lowest equity point during the Worst-case $ drawdown.
- **Number of Trades in Drawdown**: The number of trades from the start of the worst-case $ drawdown until the trade the makes a new equity high.

---

[55] Developed by Professor William R. Sharpe of Standford University.

- **Worst-case Drawdown (%)**: Largest value of the drawdowns expressed as percentage declines from the prior highest peak in equity.
- **Trade Number at Trough**: The number of the trade at the lowest equity point during the Worst-case % drawdown.
- **Number of Trades in Drawdown**: The number of trades from the start of the worst-case % drawdown until the trade makes a new equity high.

Source: *Market System Analyzer, User's Guide, Adaptrade Software, Temecula, CA. USA © 2004.*

ASSESS YOUR SYSTEM

Now that you have the statistics you need, how exactly are you going to assess your system?

When assessing the validity of your trading system, focus on the following calculations:

1. Mathematical Expectation,
2. Expected Reward,
3. Profit Factor,
4. The Sharpe Ratio,
5. Return On Account and
6. Drawdowns

MATHEMATICAL EXPECTATION (ME)

I believe that this is the most important assessment of your system, regardless of all the other methods described below. Mathematical expectation tells you whether your system is going to survive in the long run. Mathematical Expectation is defined as:

$ME = [(1 + (AW / AL)) * P] - 1$

Where   AW = Average of all your wins
                AL = Average of all your losses
                P = Probability of winning

If there is anything you should learn from this section of the book, it would be this: do not trade a system that has a negative mathematical expectation.

It has been proven that you will never be a winner in the long run if you use a trading system that has an ME of less than zero. If you want to look this up, I refer you to the following books written by Ralph Vince: *The Mathematics of Money Management* and *Portfolio Management Formulas*.

Only trade a system that shows a positive ME. When you have a system that has a positive mathematical expectation, no matter how small, you can improve its performance by using a suitable position-sizing strategy, to maximise the growth of your trading account.

You could be the most disciplined trader in the world with the ability to carry out your system flawlessly but you will still lose money in the long run if your system fails to produce a positive ME. A negative number regardless of how many times it gets multiplied will still be a negative number. You will be in the same predicament as the average gambler in a casino. Unless you are a professional who knows a way to cheat without getting caught, the mathematics are stacked against you.

EXPECTED REWARD (ER)

Having a positive mathematical expectation means having a positive expected reward. If you have total net profit data, you may use the following instead:

ER = Total Net Profit / Total Number of Trades

Sunny Harris, in her book: *Trading 102*[56], suggests calculating Expected Reward (ER) using the formula below:

ER = (PW * AW) − (PL * AL)

Where ER = Expected Reward,
PW = Probability of Winning,
AW = Average Win,
PL = Probability of Losing,
AL = Average Loss.

These two formulas give you what you can expect to earn in an average trade by trading your system. The implications of this formula are numerous. To ensure that your system keeps a positive mathematical expectation when you are optimising it, you need to remember the following ideas:

- The probability of winning needs to increase if your average win decreases in size.
- Conversely, the probability of losing must decrease if your average loss increases in size.
- Your average win needs to increase in size if your likelihood of winning reduces.
- Conversely, your average loss may increase if the likelihood of losing reduces.

PROFIT FACTOR (PF)

This tells us how many dollars we gain for every dollar we lose. This value must be greater than 1. If it is less than 1, you will lose money.

---

[56] Who in turn, got the formula from *Money Management Strategies for Futures Traders* by Nauzer J Balsara.

THE SHARPE RATIO

Simply put, the Sharpe Ratio is a measure of risk adjusted return. Higher Sharpe Ratios are better. This is one of the generally-accepted methods of comparing the performances of traders and fund managers.

DRAWDOWNS

In looking at the drawdown figures, you need to take a look at your maximum drawdown as well as your average drawdown over the entire duration of your sample data. The limitations of your money management strategy will rely a lot on this, as we shall soon see in the chapter related to position-sizing.

CHAPTER 14: POSITION-SIZING

DISTINGUISHING BETWEEN POSITION-SIZING, RISK-MANAGEMENT & MONEY MANAGEMENT

Position-sizing, risk-management and money management are often used interchangeably in trading. It is usually acceptable to use one term for another. However, there are subtle differences in the context in which they can be used.

A position-sizing strategy tells you how much money you will be committing on each trade. Would you be buying 100 shares or 1,000 shares? Would you be buying 10,000 units of a currency or 20,000 units?

If you have a good position-sizing strategy, you are minimising your losses, which in turn will minimise your drawdowns. This is why, if you have a good position-sizing strategy, it means that you also have a good risk-management strategy.

In addition, by having a good position-sizing strategy, you will be maximising your profits to increase the growth of your trading account. This is why having a good position-sizing strategy suggests that you have a good money management strategy as well.

POSITION SIZING IS YOUR ARMOUR

Your trading system is the weapon you use to engage the market. You could have a powerful weapon but when you do not have armour, any minor mistake can lead to your flesh being ripped apart. In trading, risk-management is that armour. Without it, you are exposed to danger.

There are many traders who feel that putting stop-losses is enough to pass as a risk-management strategy. Having a sound risk-management is not just about putting a stop-loss order to limit your losses when your trade goes bad. A sound strategy dictates why, where and how you put stop-loss levels in the first place. It is a logical approach that you apply consistently, trade after trade.

Position-sizing is a balancing act. If you trade too small, your losses from the bad trades will be smaller, but at the same time, your profits from the good trades will be smaller as well. Your account will take a while to grow. Conversely, if you trade too big, your profits will be bigger. However, when you lose, your losses will be big enough to cripple your account's capacity to gain your money back. Position-sizing will be the key factor in whether you stay long enough to be a trader. It is that crucial.

THE IMPORTANCE OF TRADING SMALL POSITIONS

Consider this: Let's say you have $10,000 in your margin account. If you risk a certain percentage of your account per trade, how many consecutive times can you be wrong before your account shrinks to a mere $100?

For this exercise, let us assume that your broker allows you to trade a minimum contract size of a dollar. This implies that you can control exactly how much you are willing to risk per trade, because you can trade almost any amount you want.

The table below shows that if you only risk 1% in every trade, you can make 459 losing trades in a row before your $10,000 account shrinks to $100. If you risk 2% per trade, you can risk losing 228 times in a row. If you risk 20% per trade, you can only afford 21 consecutive losses and the chances are high that you will not stay long enough to play in the market.

The relationship between the risks you take per trade and the number of consecutive losses you can make before diminishing your account is tabulated as follows:

Risk (%)	1	2	3	4	5	6	7	8	9	10
Trades	459	228	152	113	90	75	64	56	49	44
Risk (%)	11	12	13	14	15	16	17	18	19	20
Trades	40	37	34	31	29	27	25	24	22	21

And graphically, it looks like this:

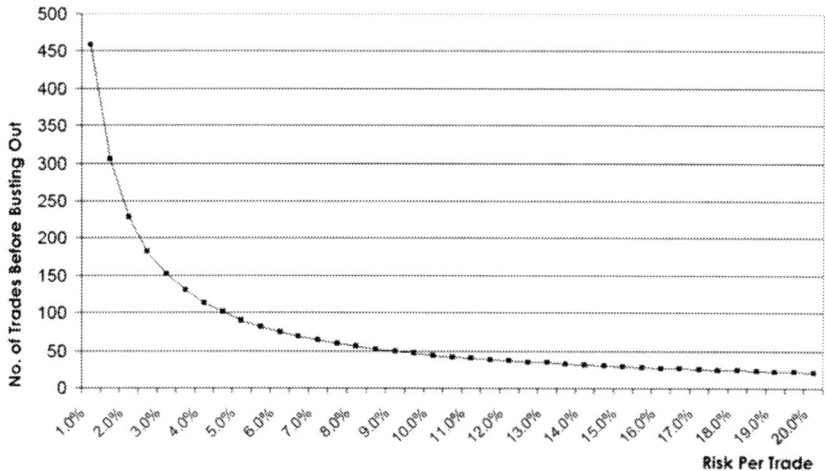

Image 65: Risk Per Trade Vs. Number Of Trades Before Busting Out

As you can see, you can reduce the risks of ruin simply by trading small sizes. The message is simple: Do not trade too much. By reducing your trade size, you are effectively buying yourself more time to be in the market to learn as much as you can.

Despite knowing how crucial it is to trade small sizes, you may still find yourself risking too much occasionally. It happens. You get excited because for one reason or another, you think the next trade is going to be a big trade. Perhaps you may have just learnt something new or you have just improved your system. Regardless of what it could be, you end up putting on a big position. Instead of buying 10,000 units of a currency, you buy

$50,000, which is five times what you normally would trade. You only look forward making five times your money but then, what happens? The trade ends up being a loser...a loser five times as big! Therefore, in those moments when you feel most confident, watch out. It is ironic how often a trader increases his risk when he should be reducing it.

When I started trading, a veteran trader told me to conduct each trade as if it were the first trade I make out of a million trades in my entire life. He instilled in me that a novice trader should expect to make millions of mistakes when he begins. "If you last long enough, the money will come", he said.

It was that early warning that saved me from wiping out any of my trading accounts. For all traders, there will be countless times when the temptation of putting on a big position becomes very strong, especially when big profits are anticipated. Often, it ends with devastating results.

During your early days of trading, how much is small enough? The best traders and investors in the world commented on the subject of risk-management in interviews with Jack Schwager, published in the books: *Market Wizards* and *The New Market Wizards*. According to them, risk-management is the most important aspect of trading. It needs to be well understood. From having read the books, let me summarise the overall impression I got: risk as little as 1% of your trading account. If you can, risk less.

WHAT 'THE 1% RULE', MEANS

What does it mean to risk only 1% of your account per trade? Many people assume that if they have $10,000 in their trading accounts, they can only trade $100 of a currency. This is not what it means. Let me explain by using an example.

Image 66: The 1% Rule Example

Here is an example:

- A trader is trading the 1 hour chart of the EUR/USD.
- A resistance level has just been broken and the trader enters a trade. This entry is marked by the white arrow on the chart.
- He wants to put a stop-loss at 1.1946, so if the market goes downwards, he exits the trade at that level.
- When he exits, he wants his loss to be no more than 1% of his equity.

QUESTION:
How many Euros should he buy so when he loses, he only loses 100 USDs?

ANSWER:
He should buy 20,833 EURs. (I will show you how this is calculated further on.)

To prove that this is right, we use the formula from Chapter 3, to calculate the profits gained from a trade in terms of the quote currency.

$$P = U(S - B)$$

Where:
P = Profit is expressed in terms of the Quote Currency of the currency pair we are trading. So if we are trading the USD/JPY, P will be expressed in terms of JPYs.
U = Units to Trade
S = Selling Price
B = Buying Price

We substitute the values:
P = 20833*(1.1946 − 1.1994)
P = -100 ← It is a negative number because it is a loss.

This proves that if the trader buys 20,833 EURs and the trade closes at his stop-loss, his loss is no more than 100 USDs.

Therefore, the 1% rule does not mean that you can only have a position size of 100 USDs worth of EURs. In fact, you can buy 20,833 EURs which is worth 24,887 USDs and still only lose 100 USDs if the trade hits your stop-loss level. The 1% rule only means that you can only lose 1% of your account whenever you have a bad trade.

For those readers who still do not understand the concept of margin trading at this point, you do not need to have 24,887 USDs in your trading account to buy 20,833 EURs. You get 'lent' the money. Please refer to Chapter 3 on the topic of margin lending because it is important in currency trading. Failure to understand this is damaging to your trading account.

I will now show you how I arrived at the 20,833 EURs.

HOW TO CALCULATE YOUR POSITION SIZE

Considering the importance of risk-management, I find it alarming that – at the time of writing – many brokers do not provide their customers adequate tools needed to calculate their risks. Therefore, if you use one of those brokers, let me show you how you can calculate the size of your positions to ensure that you do not risk more than 1% of your total account when you lose. After understanding the method, you can formulate it in a spreadsheet to automate most of the calculations for you.

The formula to calculate your position size according to your maximum risk is:

$$R * S = U * (S - B)$$

Or similarly,

$$U = (R * S) / (S - B)$$

Where:
R = Your maximum **risk** expressed in terms of the quote currency;
S = **Selling price**: where you will be putting a stop-loss;
B = **Buying price**: where you will be opening your trade;
U = **Units to Trade** which is expressed in the base currency of the pair you wish to trade. It does not matter if this is a positive or a negative number, all that matters is the number. For example, if it equals (− 15000), you just open a position size of 15,000 of the Base currency of the currency pair you will trade.

Here are the steps to calculate R:

Step 1: Calculate your risk in terms of your home currency by multiplying your total account balance with your risk percentage. Risk factor is 1% if you do not want to lose more than 1% of your account each time you lose.

Step 2: Convert your risk from your home currency to the base currency of the currency pair that you are trading. To do this, you multiply the amount from step 1 by the exchange rate of your home currency over the base currency of the currency pair that you are trading.

Alternatively, both steps can be expressed as shown:

R = AccountBalance * RiskFactor * ExchangeRate $_{\text{HomeCurrency | BaseCurrency}}$

EXAMPLE 1: When the home currency is one of the currencies in the currency pair you wish to trade

CALCULATION METHOD 1

We use the same example as above.

- We are trading EUR/USD with 10,000 USDs in our trading account and we risk no more than 1% of that, every time we lose.
- Our home currency is USD.
- We are entering at 1.1994,
- We are exiting at 1.1946, if it hits our stop-loss.

First, we calculate R:

R = AccountBalance * RiskFactor * Exchange Rate $_{\text{HomeCurrency | BaseCurrency}}$

R = 10,000 * 0.01 * Exchange Rate $_{\text{USD | EUR}}$

R = 100 * 0.8371 ← We need to find the exchange rate between our Home Currency and the Base Currency. Our home currency is USD. The base currency of the EUR/USD is EUR. Therefore, the exchange rate we need is that of USD/EUR[57]. We know that EUR/USD = 1.1946; therefore, USD/EUR = 0.8371[58].

R = 83.71

---

[57] Remember, in this book we are using the Indirect Quotation method. (*See Chapter 5.*)
[58] 1 / 1.1946 = 0.8371.

Next, we calculate U:

U = (R * S) / (S – B)
U = (83.71 * 1.1946) / (1.1946 – 1.1994)
U = 100 / –0.0048
U = – 20833 EURs ← We buy 20,833 Euros. Ignore the negative (–) sign.

CALCULATION METHOD 2

Calculation Method 1 works with any currency pair. This method is a short-cut only when your home currency is the same as the quote currency of the currency pair you wish to trade. In this case, our home currency (USD) is the same as the quote currency of the currency pair we wish to trade (EUR/USD).

Using the formula, we calculate U:

P = U (S – B)
-100 = U (1.1946-1.1994)
U = – 20833 EURs ← Ignore the negative (–) sign.

EXAMPLE 2: When the home currency is not one of the currencies in the currency pair we wish to trade.

Here is another example:
- We are trading GBP/JPY hourly charts.
- We have 10,000 USDs in our trading account and we risk no more than 1% of that, every time we lose.
- We see a 'long' trade opportunity.
- We enter the market at 201.18 and we exit at 200.56 if the trade goes bad.
- We calculate how many units GBPs we should buy to ensure that if the GBP/JPY goes down, we will exit at a controlled loss of no more than 1% of our account.
- Current GPB/USD rate is 1.7782 and
- The current USD/JPY rate is 112.78.

Our chart looks like this:

Image 67: When Home Currency Is Not In The Currency Pair

First we calculate R:

R = AccountBalance * RiskFactor * ExchangeRate $_{HomeCurrency\ |\ BaseCurrency}$

R = 10000 * 0.01 * ExchangeRate $_{USD\ |\ GBP}$

R = 100 * 0.5624 ← Since GBP/USD = 1.7782
 Then USD/GBP = 1/1.7782
 USD/GBP = 0.5624

R = 56.24

Next, we calculate U:

U = (R * S) / (S – B)

U = (56.24 * 200.56) / (200.56 – 201.18)

U = 11279.49 / (-0.62)

U = – 18191 GBPs ← This is our position size, we ignore the (–) sign.

This means that we open a position size of 18,191 GBPs.

To prove that our loss is going to be just 100 USD, if we buy 18,191 GBPs, we use the formula to calculate our loss:

$P = U(S - B)$
$P = 18191(200.56 - 201.18)$
$P = -11278$ JPYs ← This is our loss expressed in JPYs.

USD/JPY is 112.78; therefore, 11278 JPYs / 112.78 = 100 USDs

This means we would lose no more than 100 USDs if the trade closes at our stop-loss level.

CALCULATING POSITION SIZE IF YOU DO NOT USE STOP LOSSES

The calculation examples above require that you use stop losses in your system, because the fraction of equity you risk is based on your stop loss. If you do not use stop losses, the fraction of equity you risk can also be based on the maximum loss or the average loss of your trading system.

Traders who do use stop losses still have the option of using this method to calculate their position size. So instead of ensuring that you risk no more than 1% of your equity if the market hits your stop loss, you can ensure that you risk no more than 1% of your equity if the next trade is equal to your system's maximum loss or average loss in the past.

RISK-MANAGEMENT STRATEGIES

When you begin trading other people's money and you have a sizeable amount of investors' funds in your trading account, then you may have enough to divide them between different instruments and different markets. By that time, you may need complex risk-management strategies to allow you to diversify your funds effectively between many markets and many instruments.

For now, however, I will show you three risk-management strategies. Most of the complex approaches come from the concepts of these basic strategies. Therefore, if you understand how these work, you will be able to see how you can adapt them to suit your needs later.

There are three types of risk-management strategies that you may use:

1. Fixed-size position-sizing strategy,
2. Fixed-fraction position-sizing strategy and
3. Incremental strategy.

1. 'Fixed-Size' Strategy

The fixed-size strategy is the simplest strategy of them all. You simply buy the same amount of units of a currency, regardless of whether you have been winning or whether you have been losing. For a share trader you may decide to keep buying or selling the same number of shares. For a currency trader, you may decide to keep buying or selling the same units of currencies every time your system triggers a signal for you to open a trade.

This has its advantages during your first few months or years of trading. By using a fixed-size strategy, you can focus your efforts on other aspects of trading such as your system or your psychology. You should be all right just as long as you risk a tiny amount each trade.

To give you an example of what this tiny amount could be, imagine if you have a broker based in the USA. In currency trading, if you trade 100,000 units of a currency, every point the currency pair makes, affects your margin account by around 10 US Dollars. If you are trading 10,000 units of a currency, every point is worth 1 US Dollar of your margin account. If you are trading only 1,000 units of a currency, then every point is only worth 10 US cents. If you are a novice trader and your broker allows you to trade as small as 100 units, go for it. Just trade 100 units each time. This is one of the biggest reasons you should go for a broker that allows you to trade a contract size as little as one dollar. It is for your trading account's survivability.

During this stage, a novice trader should take the opportunity to prepare himself psychologically and get used to the idea of trading with real money. It is during this stage, where a novice can try trading different time-frames and start finding what he can practically commit to.

For example, if you want to trade three-hour charts, then see if you have the discipline, the stamina and the regimen to wake up every three hours at night to make your analysis and execute your trades. It is only after exploring all these aspects of trading that a novice trader should begin exploring riskier money management strategies.

2. 'Fixed-Fraction' Strategy

The 'fixed-fraction' strategy is simply risking a fraction of your remaining equity in every trade that you make. This approach is logical in a sense that if your account is diminishing, it suggests that there are still aspects of your trading you need to rectify. It is only fitting then that you reduce your risk.

Once you are trading well, you will see consistent growth in your equity balance. Fittingly, you should start trading bigger to increase the rate of growth of your account.

If you like to trade frequently, I believe that you should reduce your risk per trade from 1% to 0.25 of a percent per trade. That is not 2.5% and definitely not 25%. If a trader is able to trade less, then that would be even better. With that risk, a trader can afford to be wrong 1,840 times in a row before he busts a $10,000 account to a mere $100, assuming your broker allows you to trade very small contracts.

In my experience, trading frequently resulted in poorly-executed trades because of rushed planning. There is less time to think and learn from the previous trade and plan the next one. Therefore, giving yourself a safety net for 1,840 losses is not being overly cautious, especially when you are day-trading or when you are trading many currency pairs. However, with the gains that you make from some of your profitable trades, you may have enough time to learn enough and rescue your account before it depletes to a minuscule amount.

The priority of novice traders in their early days of trading should be to protect their account. The early years should be about making sure that they have a system that can grow money. It does not matter that their testing shows a positive mathematical expectation of success. It is only actual trading conditions that will confirm if this is true or not. It is the real world that will give traders an idea of which areas of their trading they need to work on.

As long as traders cannot see a consistent growth in their trading account, where would the wisdom be in risking more? If they cannot make 300 dollars from buying and selling 10,000 units of a currency after three months, what would make them think that they can make 3,000 by trading 100,000 units of a currency? A trader should consider risking more only after he sees a steady increase in his account balance.

3. Incremental Strategy

Traders may decide to trade using a 'fixed-size' strategy at the beginning; however, as their account grows, they increase the sizes of their positions. There are a couple of ways this can be done:

1. Increase the position size using the 'fixed-size' method incrementally and
2. Increasing the position size using the 'fixed-fraction' method incrementally.

Method 1:

Incrementally increase the position size using the fixed-size method. In this method, we increase the number of units we buy as our margin account grows. An example of how this can be done, is shown below. If a trader has between $500 and $2,000 in his account, he will be trading 1,000 units of a particular currency each trade. Once his account grows to a size between $2,001 and $5,000, he can start trading 5,000 units of a particular currency each trade. Once his equity grows to a size between $5,001 and $10,000, the trader can start trading 20,000 units of a currency each trade. The process goes on as the account grows bigger.

Margin Account Balance ($)	Position Sizes in units of currencies
500 – 2,000	1,000
2,001 – 5,000	5,000
5,001 – 10,000	20,000
10,001 – 15,000	50,000
15,001 – 20,000	100,000

Method 2:

Incrementally increase the position size using the fixed-fraction method. In this method, we risk more of our margin account as our margin account grows bigger. For example, when our account is between $500 and $2,000 we only risk 0.5% of our account per trade. When our account grows to between $2,001 and $5000 we increase our risk to 1.0% of our account per trade. When our account grows to between $5001 and $10,000, we start risking 1.5% of our total account.

Margin Account Balance ($)	Risk Factor (%)
500 – 2,000	0.5%
2,001 – 5,000	1.0%
5,001 – 10,000	1.5%
10,001 – 15,000	2.0%
15,001 – 20,000	2.5%

EXPLORING THE VARIABLES OF POSITION-SIZING

If you consider yourself to be a novice or an intermediate-skilled trader and you have not delved into the topic of position-sizing, I need you to follow me closely in the next series of examples. I may be able to uncover ideas which could be of importance to your trading now and in the future.

Let us consider the situation of a trader named Sandra:

- She has an initial margin account of $50,000.
- She has traded 10,000 size contracts each time because that is the minimum trade size her broker allows. That means that every point movement made by the currency pair she has been trading roughly equalled $1.
- She has traded 1,000 trades in a period of 6 years from this system.
- The numbers below show the basic statistics of her trading performance, which closely match the results of the tests of her trading system.
    Winning Rate: 35%
    Losing Rate: 65%
    Average Win: $200
    Maximum Win: $250
    Average Loss: $50
    Maximum Loss: $125

Using Fixed-Size Contract

Based from such numbers, here is what Sandra's margin account curve – also referred to as her equity curve – would have been like after 1,000 trades.

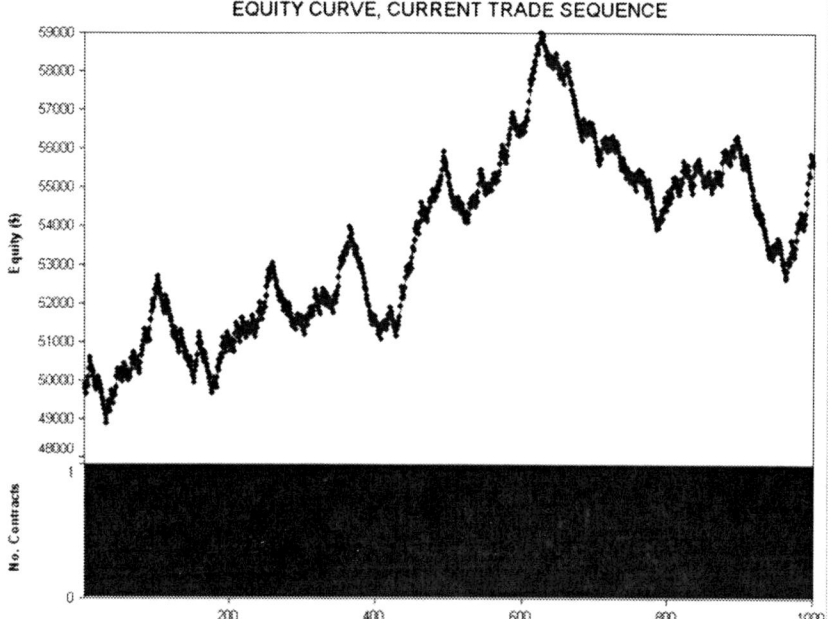
Image 68: Sandra's Equity Curve Using 1 Fixed-Size Contract

Other trading statistics not visible from this chart are:
Equity High=$58996, Equity Low=$48885, **Net Profit** =$5592, Final Equity, $55592, Return On Starting Equity=11.18%, **Average Trade**=$5.59 (0.01%), **Maximum Drawdown**=-$6359 (10.78%), Profit Factor=1.08, Return-Drawdown Ratio=1.038, Modified Sharpe Ratio=0.0365.

On this chart, we can see that Sandra has had a net profit of $5,592, an average trade of $5.59 and a maximum drawdown of 10.78%[59]. It is a good system. It spits out money. It took her six years to make $5,592 though. She was hoping that she would get to a position where she can quit her $40,000 a year job so she can trade full-time. She is now looking for a way on how she can improve her system.

Obviously, her system has a positive mathematical expectation. She has traded 1,000 times and the system did come out profitable. She has also managed to design a trading system

---

[59] To clarify what drawdown means in this example, a 10.78% drawdown means that Sandra's trading account dropped 10.78% at one point from a high peak to a low peak.

that suited her psychological make up since she was able to follow it all these years. Now that she has tried what it is like with fixed-size position-sizing, she can start playing around with a fixed-fraction strategy. That way, the size of her trades increase as her account increases as well. By doing this, she makes more money when her trades are profitable.

Let's see what happens to the original sequence of trades if every time she would risk 1% of her account on every trade instead of just trading a fixed-size contract of 10,000 each.

Fixed Fraction, Risking 1%

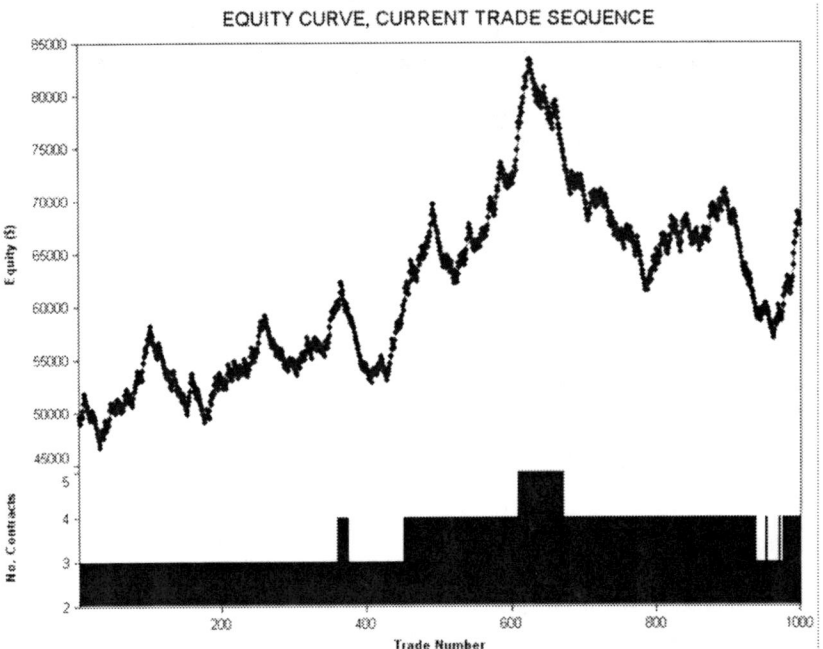

Image 69: Sarah's Equity Curve When She Risks 1% Of Her Account Per Trade

Other statistics:
Equity High=$83344, Equity Low=$46657, **Net Profit** =$17693, Final Equity, $67693, Return On Starting Equity=35%, **Average Trade**=$17.69 (0.03%), **Maximum Drawdown**=-$26339 (31.60%), Profit Factor=1.071, Return-Drawdown Ratio=1.120, Modified Sharpe Ratio=0.0368.

As you can see, her net profit increased by 316% to $17,693 and her average trade by 316% to $17.69. However, take note that her maximum drawdown has increased by 293% to 31.60%. What this shows is that the returns of a trading system that has a positive mathematical expectation can be magnified with a good position-sizing strategy. In doing so, we also worsen our drawdown.

$17,693 in six years is not bad according to Sandra. It is better than $5,592. She gets excited. She then wonders what would happen if she starts risking 10% of her total account per trade. If risking 1% increased her profitability 3 times, perhaps risking 10% would increase her profitability 30 times, she guesses.

Fixed Fraction, Risking 10%

This is what would have happened to her trading account if she risked 10% of her account per trade.

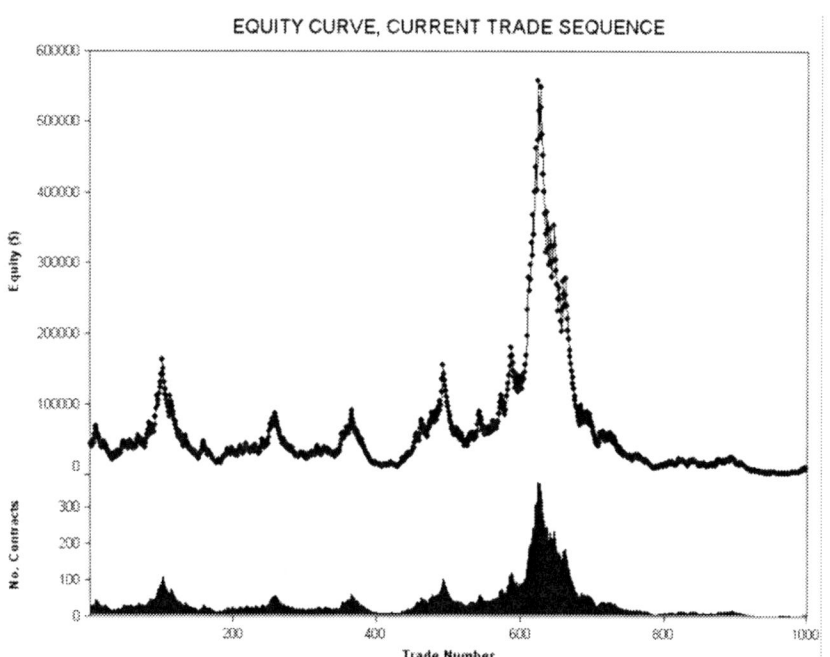

Image 70: Sarah's Equity Curve When She Risks 10% Of Her Trading Account Per Trade

Other Statistics: Equity High=$556947, Equity Low=$2549, Net Profit = –$40865, Final Equity, –$40865, Return On Starting Equity= –81.73%, Average Trade=–$40.87 (0.34%), Maximum Drawdown= –$554398 (99.54%), Profit Factor=0.986, Return-Drawdown Ratio=0.00, Modified Sharpe Ratio=0.0327.

Had she risked 10% of her account in every trade, she would have lost all her money at some time during those six years. The most important lesson in this is that even a workable system with a positive mathematical expectation can be made unprofitable, if it is traded with a risky position-sizing strategy.

Optimal Risk

Disappointed with the results above, Sandra asks what would be the maximum percentage she can risk without losing her profitability. As it turns out, to get the best results from her system, the optimum risk level[60] is 3.54% of her equity.

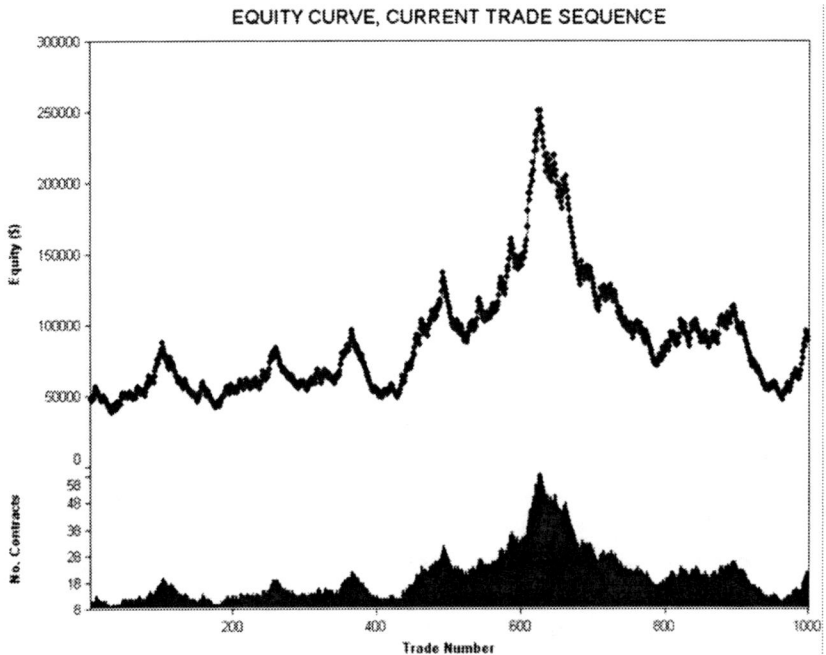

Image 71: Sarah's Optimum Equity Curve

---

[60] Based on her current trades record.

Other statistics:
Equity High=$251076, Equity Low=$38198, **Net Profit** =$39346, Final Equity, $89346, Return On Starting Equity=78.69%, Average Trade=$39.35 (0.13%), **Maximum Drawdown**=-$204031 (81.26%), Profit Factor=1.027, Return-Drawdown Ratio=0.9684, Modified Sharpe Ratio=0.0338.

The best Sandra would have been able to do, was to gain $39,346 in those six years without risking her profitability. A $39,346 (that is $6,558[61]/year) gain is a phenomenal difference from the $5,592 that she got when she traded using fixed-size contracts. By employing a good money-management strategy, her system can potentially earn seven times as much!

A $6,558 a year return was not what she was hoping for but what this shows is that a trading system has a limit. It is much like a machine. Its components can only handle so much and there is a limit to what profit level a trader can reasonably expect from his trading strategy. You should not expect a machine designed to cut paper to cut through metal as well.

Sandra must also be aware that to get this gain, she would have needed to 'stomach' a drawdown ratio of 81.26%. That would mean that at one time, her trading account balance would have dropped from one of its peaks 81% down to a trough! Unless a trader is psychologically prepared for this possibility, panic is likely to happen.

Most people would not be able to cope when their account balance declines to a mere 19% of its original size. Most will abandon the system if it does not work immediately, when in fact it would have…in the long term. This is one of the reasons why you should test your system. By testing, you can prepare psychologically for what is likely to happen in the future and not panic when it does happen.

Depending on how good Sandra is in handling drawdowns, her best risk level would be between 1% and 3.5%. She may also want to start adjusting her trading system in a way that can give her an income of $40,000 a year to replace her current salary.

---

[61] $39346 / 6 years = $6558

Summary Of Lessons

To conclude, the points to remember from this series of examples are the following:
1) The level of risks we choose directly affects our profitability, as well as our drawdown levels;
2) A profitable trading system can be made unprofitable at high risk levels and
3) Trading systems have limits to what profit they can produce.

Portfolio Analysis

From what we can gather from the series of examples above, we have three areas to be concerned about when we are using trading systems and position-sizing strategies:

1) Profitability and drawdown levels,
2) Risk and
3) Performance limitations of trading systems.

Sandra, in the example above, has a good system. Using a fitting position-sizing strategy, she can immensely increase her profitability. However, with the limitations of her trading system, even the best position-sizing strategy is not going to get her to her dream of letting go of her $40,000-a-year job very soon.

Apart from adjusting her trading system, she may also begin to explore the idea of trading a set of different currencies, different markets and different instruments to take advantage of her system. This way, she may find ways to increase her profitability, reduce her drawdown levels, maintain her risks or perhaps even reduce them, despite the performance limitations of her trading system.

The topic of portfolio analysis however, is beyond the scope of this book. A good resource to start off in this train of thought would be the books written by Ralph Vince: *The Mathematics of Money Management* and *Portfolio Management Formulas*.

CHAPTER 15: DISCIPLINE & PSYCHOLOGY

When money is involved, people get emotional. That is why trading is such an emotional activity. It is not because money is evil, as some of us might say, but rather because it represents the value of everything a person sacrifices to earn it. Even some successful professional traders have difficulty repeating their performances when they quit their jobs and begin trading their own money. The generally-accepted explanation to this is attributed to the belief that they become more emotional when their own money is involved.

People experience the emotions of fear and greed when they trade. For example, a trader may not cut his losses because doing so would be like admitting that he has made a mistake. His mistake would be certified as a loss in his transaction records. He will delay in closing the trade because as long as it is open, there is always a chance the market will turn around, giving him the chance to redeem his ego.

In another case, a trader may sometimes open a trade in haste, without waiting for a valid signal from his system and without making sufficient analysis. He fears that he will miss what is going to be the biggest trade of the decade: the one that will make him rich.

Another trader may not take his profits when he is supposed to. He believes the more money he can 'squeeze out' of the current trade, the more he can make up for the losses he has incurred in the past. In an exactly opposite example, a trader may choose to close a trade too soon, with a tiny gain, because he is afraid the market will reverse and take away his open profits.

A trader may be able to develop the best trading system and couple it with the most suitable position-sizing strategy, but all the planning, research and testing will go to waste if he cannot follow his system in the end. I believe that in life – as well as in trading – success goes to the individuals who have the discipline to do exactly what they know they should be doing.

HOW AND WHY DO TRADERS DISOBEY THEIR SYSTEM?

To understand our predicament as traders, we need to recognise that it is not only the lack of discipline that is the problem. We need to identify all the stuff within us and in our lives that impact on our ability to obey our trading rules.

Traders disobey their systems because of the reasons below:

1. Operational problems,
2. Financial pressure,
3. Psychological issues and
4. Health and life issues.

1) **Operational Problems**

These problems are associated to the trader's lack of skills and knowledge: problems that get in the way of running his trading business competently. These problems include the following:

a. A trader lacking sufficient knowledge of the markets, of trading and of his behaviour;
b. A trader lacking the skills he needs to test his systems appropriately: including programming skills, mathematical skills and computer skills;
c. A trader making wrong assumptions and judgments of the market, the nature of trading and of himself;

d. A trader getting confused about how he should be carrying out his system. The confusion is likely because his rules are not clear and specific enough;
e. A trader having a system that has too many discretionary rules. It requires his analysis and input. This increases the chance for his emotions to interfere with his trading decisions;
f. A trader getting overwhelmed with the number of tasks he has to do and as a result, he falls behind because of slack organisational and planning skills;
g. A trader confusing himself about what timeframe he should be trading;
h. A trader confusing himself with conflicting messages that are signalled by different indicators;
i. A technical analyst trying to include fundamental analysis in his trading methods;
j. A trader allowing his trading decisions to be affected by other people;
k. A trader not following his system because it does not match his personality;
l. A trader not following his system because it does not fit well in his daily routines;
m. A trader not setting stop-losses and his take-profit levels consistently.
n. A trader not opening a trade that his system signals him to;
o. A trader opening trades too early before his system gives him a signal;
p. A trader opening trades too late way after his system gives him a signal;
q. A trader not taking profits even if his system tells him to and
r. A trader not limiting his losses when his system is telling him to.

2) Financial and Career-Related Pressure

Financial and career-related pressures include the following:

a. A trader using position sizes that are too big relative to the size of his account, because he is undercapitalised or because he is willing to take on higher risks;
b. A trader using position sizes that are too small to keep him from getting bored and this could result in him taking on unplanned trades;
c. A trader breaking his rules because of his desperation and his need for money to provide him with what he wants and needs;
d. A trader breaking his rules because he feels pressured to prove to himself and to impress others that he is making money from trading;
e. A trader trading too much because he wants to get rewarded fast and quick;
f. A trader treating trading like a gambling activity where he hopes to make a fortune overnight;
g. A trader spending too much money beyond his means hoping that trading can take care of his financial shortage and
h. A trader opening trades not for the validity of those trades, but to make himself feel he has a career direction.

3) Psychological issues

Examples of psychological issues are listed below:

a. A trader trading dangerously for the excitement he gets from the activity;
b. A trader procrastinating in doing what he needs to do to excel in his trading;
c. A trader lacking motivation;

d. A trader who, being a perfectionist, never starts trading;
   e. A trader lacking confidence. This can be obvious from:
      i. His inability to take action because he does not trust himself and his system,
      ii. Fear of failure,
      iii. Fear of losing money,
      iv. Fear of being wrong,
      v. Fear of success,
      vi. His greediness and
      vii. His constant habit of breaking his rules.
   f. A trader fearing what he expects the future to bring including:
      i. Fear of having success that can be taken away,
      ii. Fear of success and what it might bring and
      iii. Fear of not being able to trade in the future.
   g. A trader being continuously in an emotional state that is not helpful to his trading, states like:
      i. Anger,
      ii. Guilt,
      iii. Worry and
      iv. Anxiety.
   h. A trader engaging in undermining his success because of his belief that he is undeserving or unworthy of success. He makes it a habit to be critical of himself and his worth most of the time.

4) Physical Health and Life Issues

Physical health and life-related issues include the following:

   a. A trader's performance being affected when he undergoes exciting changes in his life including getting married, getting a new job, having a newborn child or buying a house;
   b. A trader's performance being affected when he undergoes distressing events like death, divorce and bankruptcy;

c. A trader's unhealthy lifestyle and habits having the potential of interfering with his ability to trade well;
   d. A trader feeling that he is not being rewarded for all his hard work;
   e. A trader not communicating enough with his loved ones that he risks being misunderstood and being denied the support he needs and
   f. A trader trading to give meaning to his life.

THE MINDSET OF A TRADER

To overcome many of these problems, traders need to understand how they operate, so they can develop those aspects of themselves where improvements are needed. For some people, the origins of their problems are deeply rooted within their psyche and professional help is essential. Usually however, the problems in trading are all products of only one, or just a few, causes that a trader may be able to identify on his own. Once a trader identifies what it is about himself that complicates his efforts, the impact of most of his trading problems will diminish. In my early days of trading, I struggled with many of these difficulties. It had not been until I managed to become aware of my thinking and my behaviour when pieces of what seemed like a big jigsaw puzzle, began to lock in. I will share with you the lessons I have learnt along the way and I hope they will alleviate most of the difficulties experienced by some of you, who are reading this.

I have learnt that most of the problems listed above are mainly because of the following reasons:

1) A trader lacks confidence in himself and in his system;
2) A trader does not understand the impact of position-sizing on his emotions and psychology and
3) A trader is not focused because he does not know, or he forgets, what his sole objective is, since his judgment is clouded by his financial, emotional and psychological needs.

CONFIDENCE

In my trading experience, the one underlying cause for operational-related problems is the lack of confidence. If you have confidence, you will have the discipline to do what you know you should be doing. The confidence needed is not the fake one; not the one which is congruent with arrogance and ignorance. This confidence can only be gained with humility, patience and hard work. Operational-related problems are usually problems that occur because a trader does not have the confidence in his system.

If a trader does not have confidence in his system, it will make him ignore the signals that it gives. He hesitates taking action and delays opening a trade or closing a trade. By having confidence he does not have to seek the approval of other people. He does not have to listen to news or to some guru for extra guidance. If he has confidence in his system, he already knows what to do: follow his system.

The only way for a trader to trust his system is through scrutinizing, modifying and testing the robustness of it in every possible condition he can think of. If after testing his system across many different markets, different time frames and different instruments, he finds that his system wins in the end, then the trader's confidence in his system will improve. If the system tells him that out of a 1,000 trades, he can expect to win 45% of the time and gain twice as much as he does when he loses, then the trader has a positive mathematical expectation. He has a statistical 'edge'.

It will become easier to follow his system because he has already tested it. He executes his trades indifferently from one trade to another, not caring whether the next one is going to be a profit or a loss. Even if the future is never exactly like the past, the odds are on his side and he is certain: he will prevail. Soon the trader will have no problems accepting to close his trades when he has to. He will not fear what the market is going to do next because it no longer matters. He behaves as if he has already won. All he needs to do is to collect money simply by obeying his rules exactly the way he has tested them. The procedure then becomes automatic and he can do it without too much thinking and analysis. Many of the emotional difficulties including the fear of failing, fear of losing, fear of missing out and the fear of being wrong will no longer have an impact on his behaviour. This is what it means to be a confident trader.

On the other hand, if the trader knows that he did not develop and test his system in all types of market conditions, he will fear the market will present his system the type of conditions it cannot withstand. This is when he begins to second-guess his system and try to 'improvise'. He will begin opening trades and closing trades too soon, too late or not at all.

The problems that affect the trader's ability to obey and test his trading system are the following:

1) The trading system is too complex;
2) The trading system has too many discretionary rules;
3) The trading system is not clear enough;
4) A technical system is being confused with fundamental analysis;
5) The lack of skills;
6) The lack of self-trust;
7) The lack of patience and
8) The lack of action.

The Trading System Is Too Complex

Complex systems are difficult to test with computers and it would be too time-consuming to do manually. A trader needs to simplify his rules to make testing easier.

The Trading System Has Too Many Discretionary Rules

If the trading system has several rules that a trader has to interpret and consider at his own discretion, there is a risk that the trader will apply the rules inconsistently while he is testing the system. Each opportunity that a trader gets to exercise his discretion, increases the likelihood of a system confusing the individual during real-life trading conditions.

The Trading System Is Not Clear Enough

If a trader gets confused about what time frame he should be looking at, or which indicator he should be basing his decisions on, it is because he has not defined his rules clearly enough. Someone once wrote that unless you can write all the rules of your trading system on the back of a small envelope, then you do not have a trading system[62].

A Technical System Is Being Confused With Fundamental Analysis

Fundamental analysts can use technical indicators in their analysis to time their trades and vice versa. However, if a trader is trying to follow a trading system based purely on technical indicators, then the trader should not be considering any fundamental news, indicators or analysis techniques while he is in a trade. Doing so will only confuse him about what he needs to do next and it will lead him to breach his purely technical trading system.

If a trader wants to consider fundamental analysis indicators, then he has to consider the following courses of action:

1) He trades a long-term timeframe (probably monthly, half-yearly or yearly charts) and
2) He includes whatever fundamental indicator he needs to use – like the interest rate – in his trading system when he tests it and when he executes it.

---

[62] Joe Krutsinger, *The Trading Systems Toolkit (1993)*, p24

Lack Of Skills

The lack of skills is the reason some traders are not able to test their systems properly. They avoid using maths and computers to solve their problems because they do not know how to use them. If a trader has difficulties using computers to test his systems, then all he needs is to print out the charts he wants to test. With paper, ruler and a pen, he can perform the tests manually. It may take a little more time, but his patience can compensate for his lack of skills.

Lack Of Self-Trust

Some traders do not follow their system because they do not trust it. This is because they do not trust themselves to do what they need to do. They instinctively believe they could have done more to improve and test their system, but they did not. Despite this fact, they take their 'half-baked' ideas and use them to trade the markets and expect them to work. This could be due to impatience or laziness.

Lack Of Patience

"Patience is a virtue", someone once said. It is because of the lack of this virtue that some traders rush to the market, seemingly too eager to lose all their money. Traders can save most of their capital from disappearing simply by taking the time needed to test their ideas.

The Lack Of Action

Indulging in procrastination and delaying everything that needs to be done – including learning the skills and acquiring the information necessary – is a major reason some traders never get to the level of proficiency they so desperately wish for.

THE LINK BETWEEN POSITION SIZE AND EMOTION

Traders perform better when they think of ways to improve their analyses, their strategies and themselves. It is when they lose this focus, when they start diverting their attention to the amount of money they can make or lose, that they begin to disregard the importance of risk-management and position-sizing.

If the trader starts focusing on the money, he becomes impatient of the results and wants to increase his profits by trading bigger position sizes. By increasing his position size, he increases his profits and thus, increases his losses. This will have its likely consequences. By increasing the size of his trades, he increases the size of his profits and losses.

When the sizes of his profits increase, the following behaviour is likely to occur:

- He becomes more elated when he has a good trade.
- He may start behaving a little bolder and start increasing his level of risk yet again. He may keep trading bigger and bigger position sizes until a set of losing trades come along. The market will bear its teeth, sooner or later. By this time, his position size would be so big that a few losses are enough to dent his account to unrecoverable levels.
- He may begin to feel invincible and start believing that it is okay for a 'brilliant' trader to break his own rules once in a while. And since he is so 'brilliant', he might actually improve his system's performance. He becomes greedy and arrogant.
- He may begin to override the rules of his system: opening and closing trades whenever he wants. Eventually, he abandons his system.

When the sizes of his losses increase, the following behaviour is likely to occur:

- He becomes more fearful when he has a bad trade.

- If he is more fearful, he starts behaving a little too cautious and starts reducing his risk. This is not necessarily bad; however, when he wins, his wins are too small to recover the big losses he has incurred when he was feeling more elated. This will impact on the mathematical 'edge' of his system. When the winning trades come, he realises that he should be taking on bigger positions. This triggers an inconsistent application of his position-sizing strategy.
- He may begin to start trading with bigger sizes, effectively risking more. He would do this in the hope that if the next trade was big, his wins will recover most of what he has lost in the previous trades.
- He may start to have doubts in what he is doing and in his own abilities. Any existing negative self-beliefs he has will be amplified and this undermines his confidence to do what he needs to do.
- He may override the rules of his system because he becomes afraid of being wrong and of incurring losses. In an attempt to make up for past mistakes, he begins to disobey more of his own rules. He discards his system.

In conclusion, the size of your positions has a direct relationship with the emotions you experience when you are trading. The bigger your position, the more emotional you get in response to what happens in your individual trades. This will make it more likely for you to deviate from your system. This is why a trader should trade at a size where he is no longer affected emotionally by whether the next trade is going to profitable or not. This allows him to focus on his objective.

KNOW AND FOCUS ON YOUR SOLE OBJECTIVE

When I first started trading, I thought of the market as a mystical cave, with many locks, keys, tricks and deadly traps. However, inside was a magical portal where anybody could reach into, to grab from a never-ending supply of money. So whenever I needed some money, all I had to do was to go in the cave and make my way to the portal. I would reach in and grab as much money as I could stash in my pockets. Then I had to run out and try not to get injured in the process.

The market is the only place in the world where you can go and take as much money as you can. You do not even need to have any formal excuse or any good reason to deserve it. The market gives money to those who are willing and able to take it. It is like an adult version of a fairytale land where magic still happens. For speculative traders, the market serves no other purpose and it exists for us to exploit. All we have to do is to work out a way to keep on extracting money from the market without hurting ourselves. This is our task and it should be our sole focus and objective.

Simple as it may seem however, from my readings and my own trading experience, people go into the market with their financial, emotional or psychological problems. The concern arises when these problems confuse people about why they are in the market. Also, based on their various motivations to trade and their trading behaviour, it seems as though some people go to the market expecting it to mend their problems.

For example, some people are trading because of the following reasons:

a. They need money to:
- Cover their living expenses,
- Buy luxurious items,
- To fund the lifestyle they dream of,
- To quit the job they hate,
- To retire,
- To fund their child's education,
- To impress their parents,
- To impress their friends,
- To impress their neighbours,
- To impress their relatives,
- To impress previous romantic partners who have rejected them or
- To impress previous bosses who have fired them.

b. Their lives are boring and the market is an exciting place;
c. They need a career or a profession;

d. They need to show to themselves and other people that they have achieved something;
e. Their parents always wanted them to work in a similar industry and
f. Trading success can give them the affirmation they need to rectify their 'damaged' self-beliefs and they want to prove to themselves and to other people that:
  - They are worthy,
  - They deserve success,
  - They can do something right,
  - They are smart or
  - They have what it takes to be a winner.

The motivations and the justifications of why a person might be trading are not necessarily objectionable. In fact, I empathise. Nevertheless, any of these motives usually confuse the trader and as a result the trader disobeys his system. When this happens, the trader needs to re-evaluate certain expectations or misconceptions he may have about who he is and about his relationship with the market.

If a person is trading with the desperate need for money, then he must remember the market is not his bank. It does not care whether he is rich or poor. It does not give money based on the nobility of what he needs the money for and why.

When a person is trading for no other reason than to alleviate the 'boredom' or the 'senselessness' of his life, he must understand the market is not there to give meaning, excitement or entertainment to anybody's life.

If a person is trading with the burning incentive to impress himself and other people, then he is trying to solve his problems the wrong way and in the wrong place. Trading is not a solution to eradicate any doubts, fears or suspicions that he and others may have about who he is – or who he is not.

The market has no pity. The market amplifies the faults and flaws of a trader's character and reflects it to that individual in the form of severe financial devastation[63].

---

[63] For example, a trader who is trying to impress his parents or perhaps an ex-wife who believed he is not good enough, will become impatient of his system

Treating Trading As A Game

Instead of focusing on what the traders want the market to 'do' or to 'be' for them, I think the state of mind most conducive to productive trading is attained by thinking of trading as a game. By treating trading as a game, some traders would be more able to focus on the objective of winning.

If trading is a game of little consequence, then they will no longer have to set unrealistic expectations about how much money they need to make. They will no longer have the urge to take on big positions and they will start trading with small positions. By trading with small positions, they no longer have to be emotional about the outcome of every single one of their trades.

As a result, many of the emotions usually attached to trading eventually dissipate. This allows the trader to enjoy the challenges trading brings. Soon, a trader begins to set more realistic targets. As a trader reaches these targets, he becomes increasingly confident. Eventually he will start feeling excited about doing everything needed to accomplish his goals.

---

and will start trading very big positions in an attempt to get rich quickly so he can get his 'revenge'. By trading dangerously the market will present him with a loss or a series of losses that results in massive amounts of losses.

CHAPTER 16: CLOSING REMARKS

As this book approaches its close, I would like to take this opportunity to thank you, dear reader, for having read through it in its entirety. Trading can be an isolating experience and one of the reasons I did write this book is to get the chance to connect with like-minded people from all over the world.

I have written this book wanting to make it as helpful as I could for any person who wants to trade, or is already trading, the markets. I have written it with my relatives and friends in mind. I wanted to create something I would be able to take with me, back in time when I began trading, and give it to my former self during those moments of confusion and frustration.

The concepts of trading may be more complex than the concepts of other subjects. However, I do hope that I have distilled most of them in a language that conveys what I want to express, in a manner which most people find easy to read.

At some point during your reading, you might have wondered who I am. I am a private trader and I currently live in Melbourne, Australia. I started trading when I was twenty-two years old, when I was still earning my Bachelor Degree in Commerce which focused on accounting, banking and finance.

I am currently performing a sales-oriented role in one of the big telecommunication companies in Australia. I do trade part-time and that is the connection to the title of this book. I figure that if I were to be an expert at something, then it might as well be of my own circumstance. Therefore, like a character[64] in a television

---

[64] The character Kramer from the television series: *Seinfeld*.

series once said: I do 'walk' my 'talk'. For those of you who are not familiar with the metaphor, it simply implies that I do what I preach.

Trading can sometimes be exasperating. Do not force it. It becomes more difficult when you do. There are times when you probably just need a break. It is important to try and keep trading in perspective relative to everything else that you want to do in your life. For instance: I like music, so when I get the chance, I write and record my own songs. I like being an entrepreneur, taking risks to try out new ideas. I build and work with websites as a hobby and I share an online-business with my wife, Nancy, publishing art prints, books, cards and posters. I also write articles, most of which are published on my website.

What I am trying to say is that, if there are other things you want to do, my philosophy is to do them while you still can. Having picked up a book on the topic of trading and having persevered through it, tells me three things about you: (i) you are patient, (ii) you believe in self-improvement and (iii) you are highly motivated. Even though I may have never met you in person and even though you do not need luck to succeed, I do mean it with heart-felt sincerity when I say: Good luck with your trading and with any other endeavour you may decide to undertake now or in the future.

APPENDICES

APPENDIX A: IMAGES USED IN THIS BOOK

Image 1: Plotting Share Prices 23
Image 2: Plotting Forex Prices 24
Image 3: The Trading Methodology Development Process Flow Chart 68
Image 4: Close Chart 84
Image 5: HLOC Bars 85
Image 6: HLOC Bars – Group 85
Image 7: Reading Japanese Candlesticks Individually 86
Image 8: Candlesticks – Group. 86
Image 9: Expanding & Contracting Ranges 87
Image 10: Buying & Selling A Currency Pair 89
Image 11: Short-Term Bull Trends 91
Image 12: Short-Term Bear Trends 92
Image 13: Long-Term Bull Trends 93
Image 14: Long-Term Bear Trend 94
Image 15: Crab Market 95
Image 16: Trendline 98
Image 17: Accelerating Trendlines 99
Image 18: Support Levels 100
Image 19: Resistance Levels 101
Image 20: Resistance Becomes Support 102
Image 21: Support Becomes Resistance 104
Image 22: Trend Channels 106
Image 23: Entering Trades Using Classical Charting Analysis 108
Image 24: Exiting Using Classical Charting Methods – Profit 109
Image 25: Using The 'Classical' Method - Loss 110
Image 26: The Buy And Sell Signals Given By A Moving Average 114
Image 27: A 'Whipsaw' On A Moving Average 115
Image 28: Whipsaws & Shorter Moving Averages 116
Image 29: Sensitivity, Lag Effect & Whipsaws 118
Image 30: Dual Moving Average Performing In An Ideal Scenario 119
Image 31: Dual Moving Average Performing In A More Volatile Market 120
Image 32: Zero Oscillators 121
Image 33: Boundary Oscillators 121
Image 34: Bullish Oscillator Signals 122
Image 35: Zero Bullish Oscillator Signals 123
Image 36: Bullish Divergences Between Price And An Oscillator 123
Image 37: Bearish Oscillator Signals 124
Image 38: Bearish Zero Oscillator Signals 125
Image 39: Bearish Divergence Signals Between Price And An Oscillator 125

Image 40: The Stochastic Oscillator 127
Image 41: Using The Stochastic Oscillator And The Williams'%R Together .. 128
Image 42: The CCI 130
Image 43: Oscillator Sensitivity, Whipsaws & Lag Effect 131
Image 44: MACD Using Step 3 & 4 133
Image 45: MACD Using Step 5 133
Image 46: MACD Zero Trigger 134
Image 47: MACD Cross-Over Signal 134
Image 48: Zero Trigger Vs. Crossover Signals 135
Image 49: MACD Bullish Divergences 136
Image 50: MACD Bearish Divergences 136
Image 51: Example Of A Bullish MACD Divergence Signals 137
Image 52: Using Indicators Or Channels To Enter And Exit The Market 138
Image 53: Psychological Need For A Trading System 142
Image 54: Trend Trading & Counter-Trend Trading 147
Image 55: Using Stop & Limit Orders 148
Image 56: Stop-Loss Set At The Extreme Levels Of 1 Bar Ago 153
Image 57: Stop-Loss Set At The Extreme Levels Of 5 Bars Ago 154
Image 58: The Explosive Trading System In Action 160
Image 59: The Half-A-Slice Trading System In Action 162
Image 60: Trade Signals For The Shogun Trading System 164
Image 61: Stochastic Signals That The Current 'Long' Trend Is Weak 164
Image 62: Stochastic Signals That 'Short' Trade Signal Is Weak 165
Image 63: The Shogun Trading System In Action 166
Image 64: Experiment Data Layout 175
Image 65: Risk Per Trade Vs. Number Of Trades Before Busting Out 187
Image 66: The 1% Rule Example 189
Image 67: When Home Currency Is Not In The Currency Pair 194
Image 68: Sandra's Equity Curve Using 1 Fixed-Size Contract 201
Image 69: Sarah's Equity Curve When She Risks 1% Of Her Account Per Trade
.... 202
Image 70: Sarah's Equity Curve When She Risks 10% Of Her Trading Account
Per Trade 203
Image 71: Sarah's Optimum Equity Curve 204

BIBLIOGRAPHY

Beelaerts, Charles and Forde, Kevin. *You Only Profit When You Sell* (Elsternwick: Wrightbooks Pty Ltd, 2001).
Bedford, Louise. *Trading Secrets* (Milton: Wrightbooks Pty Ltd, 2005).
Douglas, Mark. *The Disciplined Trader* (New York: New York Institute of Finance, 1990).
Douglas, Mark. *Trading In The Zone* (New York: New York Institute of Finance, 2000).
Elder, Alexander. *Come Into My Trading Room* (New York: John Wiley & Sons, 2002).
Elder, Alexander. *Trading for a Living* (New York: John Wiley & Sons, 1993).
Guppy, Daryl. *Chart Trading* (Melbourne: Wrightbooks Pty Ltd, 1999).
Hamilton, W.P. *The Stock Market Barometer* (New York: John Wiley & Sons, 1998).
Harris, Sunny J. *Trading 102* (New York: John Wiley & Sons, Inc., 1998).
Headley, Price. *Big Trends In Trading* (John Wiley & Sons, Inc. New York, 2002).
Jamieson, Bill. *The Bemused Investor's Guide to Company Accounts* (Elsternwick: Wrightbooks Pty Ltd, 1997).
Krastins, I. *Listen To The Market* (Sydney: McGraw-Hill, 1991).
Krutsinger, Joe. *The Trading Systems Toolkit* (New York: McGraw-Hill, 1993).
Kiyosaki, Robert. *Rich Dad, Poor Dad* (Paradise Valley: TechPress, Inc., 1997).
Lynch Peter. *One Up on Wall Street* (New York: Simon & Schuster, 1989).
McGrath, Michael and Viney, Christopher. *Financial Institutions, Instruments and Markets* (Sydney: The McGraw-Hill Companies. Inc, 1997).
Moosa, Imad A. *International Finance* (McGraw-Hill Book Company, 1998),

Nelson, S.A. *The ABC of Stock Speculation* (Vermont: Fraser Publishing Company, 1987).

Nison, Steve. *Japanese Candlestick Charting Techniques* (New York: New York Institute of Finance, 1991).

Rhea, R. *The Dow Theory* (Vermont: Fraser Publishing Company, 1994).

Rudd, Barry. *Stock Patterns for Day Trading and Swing Trading* (Greenville: Traders Press Inc., 1998).

Schwager, Jack D. *Market Wizards* (New York: HarperBusiness, 1990).

Schwager, Jack D. *The New Market Wizards* (New York: HarperBusiness, 1992).

Slater, Robert I. *Soros* (New York: Irwin Professional Publishing, 1996).

Tate, Christopher. *Taming The Bear* (Elsternwick: Wrightbooks Pty Ltd, 1999).

Tate, Christopher. *The Art of Trading* (Elsternwick: Wrightbooks Pty Ltd, 2001).

Thomsett, Michael C. *Mastering Fundamental Analysis* (Elsternwick: Wrightbooks Pty Ltd, 1998).

Vince, Ralph. *The Mathematics of Money Management* (New York: John Wiley & Sons, 1992).

INDEX

A

ATR. *See* Average True Range
Average Drawdown, 177, 180
Average Losing Trade, 177, 179
Average Number of Trades in
  Drawdowns, 177, 180
Average Trade, 177, 179, 201, 202,
  204, 205
Average True Range, 149, 151, 152
Average Winning Trade, 177, 179

B

Bar Charts, 85
  HLOC Bars, 85
Base Currency, 24, 25, 191, 192
Bear Trend, 91, 92, 94
Bearish, 6, 79, 97, 103, 105, 106, 136,
  163, 166
Bearish Oscillator Signals, 124
Bears, 5, 74
Boundary Oscillators, 121
Break-Even Stop, 150
Bull Trend, 92, 93, 94
Bullish, 6, 79, 97, 105, 130, 136, 137,
  163, 165, 166, 167
Bullish Oscillator Signals, 122, 123
Bulls, 5, 74

C

Chart Patterns, 97, 106, 107
Classical Charting, 9, 46, 97, 107, 108,
  109, 111, 146, 147, 149, 155, 158
Close Lines, 84
Commodity Channel Index, 113, 129
Consumer Price Index, 72
Counter-Trend Trading, 108, 146
Crab Market, 95
Currency Market. See Forex Market
Curve Fitting, 167, 168

D

Dalbar, Inc., 2
Discretionary Trading Systems, 65, 145
Donald Trump, 54

E

Expected Reward, 181, 183
Explosive Trading System, The, 158
Exports, 73

F

Fibonacci Numbers, 139
Filters, 116
Final Account Equity, 177, 178
Forex Market, 14, 41, 133
Fundamental Analysis, 64, 65, 71, 72,
  73, 74, 76, 77, 79, 81, 82, 111, 144,
  173, 209, 214, 215

G

George Soros, 74
Gross Domestic Product, 72
Gross Loss, 177, 178
Gross Profit, 177, 178

H

Half-A-Slice Trading System, The, 161
Highest Closed Trade Equity, 177, 178
Home Currency, 28, 30, 40, 191, 192,
  193

I

Imports, 73
Indicators, 65, 111, 112, 117, 137, 138,
  140, 149
Initial Account Equity, 177, 178

J

Japanese Candlesticks, 86

L

Lag Effect, 117, 118, 130, 131
Largest Losing Trade, 177, 179
Largest Winning Trade, 177, 179
Leverage, 17, 20, 30, 89
Limit Orders, 148
Liquidity, 18, 56
Lowest Closed Trade Equity, 177, 178

M

MACD, 9, 113, 131, 132, 133, 134, 135, 136, 137, 156, 157, 163, 165, 166, 167, 172
Margin Account, 26, 199
Margin Lending, 7, 21, 30, 89, 190
Margin Ratio, 30, 42
Market Orders, 148
Mathematical Expectation, 181
Max Number Consecutive Losses, 179
Max Number Consecutive Wins, 179
Mechanical trading systems, 65, 145
Modified Sharpe Ratio, 177, 180, 201, 202, 204, 205
Momentum Oscillators, 113
Money Management, 46, 66, 67, 184, 185, 197
Money Supply, 72
Moving Average, 112, 129, 132, 156

N

New York Stock Exchange, 18
Number of Closed Trade Drawdowns, 177, 180
Number of Losing Trades, 178
Number of Trades in Drawdown, 177, 180, 181
Number of Winning Trades, 177, 178

O

Optimization, 168

P

Paper Trading, 173

Percent Profitable, 177, 178
Percent Risk Trailing Stop, 149
Position Size, 20, 31, 43, 89, 90, 142, 190, 191, 194, 198, 199, 217
Position-Sizing, 10, 32, 42, 45, 46, 66, 67, 145, 182, 184, 185, 196, 200, 202, 203, 204, 206, 208, 212, 217, 218
price, 15, 18, 20, 133
Price
　indicates exchange rate, 5
　indicates share price, 5
　indicates value, 5
　of a currency, 24
　Psychology impacts on price, 78
Price Quotation. *See* Indirect Quotation
Producer Price Index, 72
Profit Factor, 177, 178, 181, 201, 202, 204, 205

Q

Quantity Quotation. *See* Indirect Quotation
Quote Currency, 25, 29, 189, 191, 193

R

Rate Of Return, 72, 180
Resistance Levels, 101
Return On Account, 181
Return on Starting Equity, 177, 178
Return/Drawdown Ratio, 177, 180
Risk-Management Strategy, 66, 158, 185, 186
Robert Kiyosaki, 54

S

Sample Size, 175
Sentiment-Based Oscillators, 120
Shogun Trading System, The, 163
Spot Market, 24
Spot Rate Quotation
　Direct Quotation, 25
　Indirect Quotation, 25, 192
Spread, 27, 35, 41
Stochastic Oscillator, 113, 127, 128, 163, 164, 165, 166
Stop Orders, 148
Stop-Loss, 32, 149, 150, 151, 152, 153, 154, 155, 156, 157, 159, 161, 165

Stop-Loss Orders, 32
Support Levels, 99, 100

T

Take-Profit Mechanism, 150
Technical Analysis, 8, 46, 64, 71, 74, 76, 81, 82, 91, 97, 111, 158, 173
The Range, 87
The Sharpe Ratio, 181
Timeframe, 83, 85, 130, 131, 161, 209, 215
Total Net Profit, 177, 178, 182
Trade Number at Trough, 177, 180, 181
Trade Standard Deviation, 177, 179
Trading
   a game for the highly intellectual, 56
   for boredom, 220
   is a craft, 2
   is a game, 221
   is a hard skill to master, 2
   is a useless profession, 51
   is about the money, 51
   is about understanding many factors, 145
   is dangerous, 32, 51, 54
   is deceptively easy, 49
   is easy, 51, 58
   is emotional, 207
   is for men only, 51
   is fun and exciting, 51
   is hard, 51, 54
   is hard to master, 63
   is hazardous to your wealth, 2
   makes bankcruptcy inevitable, 2
Trading Account, 26
Trading System, 9, 10, 40, 46, 52, 64, 65, 66, 67, 68, 141, 142, 144, 145, 146, 147, 150, 155, 156, 158, 160, 162, 163, 164, 166, 167, 168, 169, 173, 174, 176, 178, 181, 182, 186, 200, 201, 203, 205, 206, 208, 214, 215, 216
Trend Channel, 105, 106
Trend Trading, 147
Trend-following Indicators, 112, 117
Trendline, 97, 98, 99, 105, 106

U

Undercapitalization, 59

V

Volatility, 19, 20, 41, 151

W

Whipsaw, 114, 115, 116, 138, 161
Williams%R, 113
Win/Loss Ratio, 177, 179, 180
Worst-case Drawdown, 180, 181

Z

Zero Oscillators, 121

Printed in the United States
133594LV00001B/172/A